The Weather and Shipping Forecast

Capt. J. Argintxona

eman ta zabal zazu

Universidad del País Vasco
servicio editorial

Euskal Herriko Unibertsitatea
argitalpen zerbitzua

ISBN: 84-8373-436-2
Depósito legal/Lege gordailua: BI - 1.426-02

Fotocomposición/Fotokonposizioa: Ipar, S. Coop.
Particular de Zurbaran, 2-4 - 48007 Bilbao

Impresión/Inprimatzea: Itxaropena, S.A.
Araba Kalea, 45 - 20800 Zarautz

The Weather and Shipping Forecast

Índice

Foreword
"Bad weather may cost lives"

This book is the outgrowth of lecture notes prepared by Capt. J. Argintxona at the Bilbao Nautical School "Bilboko Nautikako eta Itsasontzi Makinetako Goi Eskola Teknikoa".

These pages have been compiled as a book of elementary knowledge for the young officer who may think that there is a special kind of English which is used only in weather and shipping forecasts.

The book is intended to be used with the cassette that has been recorded from BBC, CNN and SKY, under prevalent sea conditions. We are here dealing with two varieties of English that are at the disposal of any user of the language.

The author wishes to acknowledge the assistance given by his colleagues Mr. Jesús Urbizu Larrazábal and Dr. Mercedes Herrera Arnaiz.

Introduction

This book is intended to give you practice in the understanding of Weather and Shipping Forecasts. It is not a book to read from cover to cover in one go; it is not even a book to start at the beginning and to progress through page after consecutive page. It is rather a book to be read and studied a little at a time, but often and regularly. How you use the book, and in what order you do the exercises, is up to you.

I would suggest that to begin with you read and listen to some of the text, don´t try to read and listen to all the section at once though. It would be better to read and listen for ten minutes or so every day than race through in one go, making sure you really understand what is written and recorded.

I have included a key to the exercises at the end of the book so that you can check your work after each exercise. There is no point in rushing through the whole section at break-neck speed and then forgetting everything two or three days later. Take one exercise at a time and work on it carefully.

J. Argintxona

Chapter 1

The Shipping Forecast

And now the Shipping Forecast, issued by the Met. Office at 23-58 on Monday the 3rd of March.

There are warnings of gales in Shannon, Rockall, Malin, Hebrides, Bailey, Fair Isle, Faeroes, and South East Iceland.

General Synopsis at 18-00, low 400 miles, Southwest of Iceland, 950, will move slowly North expected 946 by 18-00 on Tuesday. Small low East Sole, 1019, expected West Wales 1021 by the same time.

The Area Forecast for the Next 24 Hours

Viking, North Utsire, South Utsire, Forties,
Westerly backing Southerly 5 to 7, showers at first, good.

Cromarty,
Southwest 4 or 5, backing South 6 or 7, mainly fair, good.

Forth, Tyne, Dogger,
Southwest 4, backing South or Southeast 5 or 6, fair, good.

Fisher, North German Bight,
West 5 to 7, backing South 4, showers at first, good.

South German Bight, Humber,
Southwest 4, backing Southeast 5 or 6, rain later, mainly good.

Thames, Dover,
East 2, increasing 4 or 5, then veering Southwesterly, occasional rain, good becoming moderate with fog patches.

Wight, Portland, Plymouth,
Southwesterly 4 or 5 but Easterly 5 or 6 at first in North, occasional rain, moderate with fog patches, becoming good in Plymouth.

Biscay,
Variable mainly Southwesterly 3 or 4, occasional drizzle in Northwest, moderate with fog patches in Northwest.

Trafalgar,
Easterly 4 occasionally variable in North, but Easterly 7 near Gibraltar fair, moderate or good.

Finisterre,
Southwesterly 4 occasionally 5, drizzle at times, moderate occasionally poor.

Sole,
Cyclonic becoming Southwesterly 4 or 5 increasing 7 in West, rain at times, moderate, occasionally poor.

Lundy, Fastnet,
Northeasterly 5 or 6, becoming cyclonic, then Southwesterly 4 or 5, rain at times, poor becoming good.

Irish Sea,
Easterly 2 increasing 4 or 5, then varying Southerly, mainly fair, mainly good.

Shannon,
Northeast 5 in far Southeast at first, otherwise Southerly 4, increasing 6 to gale 8, mainly fair, good.

Rockall, Malin, Hebrides,
Southwest backing South 6 to gale 8, occasionally severe gale 9 in Rockall and Hebrides but 4 at first in Southeast Malin, showers, rain later, good becoming moderate.

Bailey,
South or Southwest gale 8 to storm 10, rain, moderate.

Fair Isle,
West 6, backing South 6 to gale 8, showers, then rain, good becoming moderate.

Faeroes,
South or Southwest gale 8 to storm 10, rain, moderate or poor.

Southeast Iceland,
South or Southwest gale 8 to storm 10, veering Westerly 6 later in West, rain, wintry showers later in West, moderate or poor becoming good in West.

Now,

The Weather Reports from Coastal Stations for 23.00 GMT

Tiree: Southwest 3, 16 miles, 1027, now falling.

Stornoway:Southwest 4, 22 miles, 1024, rising slowly.

Lerwick: Southwest by West 5, recent showers, 13 miles, 1019, rising slowly.

Fifeness: Southwest 3, 11 miles, 1029, rising slowly.

Bridlington: Southwest by West 1, 11 miles, 1031, falling more slowly.

Sandettie Light Vessel Automatic: East by North 5, 2 miles, 1031, falling slowly.

Greenwich Light Vessel Automatic: East 5, 2 miles, 1028, falling slowly.

Jersey: South 3, mist, 2 miles, 1026, falling slowly.

Channel Light Vessel Automatic: East Southeast 4, 1025, falling slowly.

Scilly Automatic: South Southwest 4, 600 meters, 1019, falling slowly.

Valentia: Calm, 32 miles, 1029, rising slowly.

Ronaldsway: North by East 2, 11 miles, 1031, falling slowly.

Malinhead: South Southwest 3, 19 miles, 1029, rising more slowly.

And now here is,

The Weather Forecast for the Inshore Waters of Great Britain and Northern Ireland until 18.00, today Tuesday the 4th of March

Large low will persist near Greenland, small low will move from sea area Sole to Cardigan Bay.

From Berwick upon Tweed to the Humber Estuary,
Wind, variable 2, becoming Southeasterly 4, fair, visibility moderate with fog patches at first.

From the Humber Estuary to the Isle of Wight,
Wind, Easterly 3, increasing 4 or 5, then veering Southwesterly, rain, spreading North, visibility good becoming moderate with fog patches.

From the Isle of Wight to Cardigan Bay,
Wind. Easterly 5 or 6, veering Southwesterly 4 or 5, occasional rain, visibility moderate with fog patches becoming mainly good.

From Cardigan Bay to Portpatrick including Carlinford Lough to Larne,
Wind, variable 2, becoming Southeasterly 4, occasionally 5, mainly fair, visibility mainly good but fog patches at first.

From Portpatrick to Ardnamurchan Point including Larne to Lough Foyle,
Wind, Southwest 3 or 4, backing South 5 or 6, fair, visibility good.

From Ardnamurchan Point to Duncansby Head, including the waters around Orkney and Shetland,
Wind, West or Southwest 5 to 7, backing South, increasing gale 8 later around outer Minches, mainly fair, visibility good.

finally from,

Duncansby Head to Berwick upon Tweed,
Wind, Southwest 3 or 4, backing Southeast 5 or 6 but remaining mainly force 3 in sheltered firths, fair, visibility good.

On to the final round of Weather Reports from Coastal Stations for 23.00 GMT.

Boulmer: West by South 3, 16 miles, 1030, rising more slowly.

Bridlington: Southwest by West 1, 11 miles, 1031, falling more slowly.

Sheerness: At 21-00 GMT, East Southeast 4, intermittent slight rain, 9 miles.

St. Catherine´s Point: East by North 5, continuous moderate rain, 6 miles, 1027, falling.

Scilly Automatic: South Southwest 4, 600 meters, 1019, falling slowly.

Milford Haven: East Southeast 3, 5 miles, 1026, falling more slowly.

Averporth: East 3, 11 miles, 1027, falling.

Bailey: Northeast by East 2, 19 miles, 1029, falling more slowly.

Ronaldsway: North by East 2, 11 miles, 1031, falling slowly.

Larne: At 21-00 GMT, calm, 11 miles.

Machrihanish: East by North 2, 9 miles, 1029, now falling.

Stornoway: Southwest 4, 22 miles, 1024, rising slowly.

Lerwick: Southwest by West 5, recent showers, 13 miles,1019, rising slowly.

Wick Automatic: Southwest 3, 1024, rising slowly.

Aberdeen: Southwest by West 1, 16 miles, 1027, now falling.

and finally,

Leuchars: Southwest 3, 16 miles, 1028, now falling.
and that's the end of the Shipping Bulletin.

EXERCISES

A. True or False Statements

After carefully listening to the area forecast, study the following sentences and state whether they are true or false according to the passage.

		T	F
1.	There are gale warnings in force for Rockall and Faeroes.	☐	☐
2.	There is a low of 950 mb 400 miles away from South Iceland.	☐	☐
3.	The pressure for West Wales is 1015 mb.	☐	☐
4.	The visibility for South German Bight is poor.	☐	☐
5.	The area of Biscay can expect good visibility.	☐	☐
6.	Finisterre can expect a dry day.	☐	☐

B. Weather Expected

Before sailing, a mariner should check the latest weather conditions. Try to assess the weather conditions in the following zones:

Thames, and Dover

. . . .

. . . .

. . . .

Irish Sea

. . . .

. . . .

. . . .

Fair Isle

. . . .

. . . .

. . . .

C. **Vocabulary Understanding**

With the help of a dictionary explain the meaning of the following weather-related terms.

Monsoon

. . . .

. . . .

Frontal Boundary

. . . .

. . . .

Gusty Wind

. . . .

. . . .

Storm, Heavy Rain, Showers

. . . .

. . . .

Tropical Disturbance

. . . .

. . . .

Thunderstorms

. . . .

. . . .

High Pressure Ridge

. . . .

. . . .

D. **Weather Report Form Filling**

Fill in the weather report form provided on the next page, for the following adjacent areas. 1: Cromarty, Forth, Tyne. 2: Thames, Dover, Wight. 3: Shannon, Rockall, Malin.

R. MET.SOC. / R.Y.A. METMAP (Revised Feb 1986)

GENERAL SYPNOSIS at . . . . GMT/BST . . . .

Gale	SEA AREA FORECAST		Wind	Weather	Visibility
	Viking				
	N. Utsire				
	S. Utsire				
	Forties				
	Cromarty				
	Forth				
	Tyne				
	Dogger				
	Fisher				
	German Bight				
	Humber				
	Thames				
	Dover				
	Wight				
	Portland				
	Plymouth				
	Biscay				
	Finisterre				
	Sole				
	Lundy				
	Fastnet				
	Irish Sea				
	Shannon				
	Rockall				
	Malin				
	Hebrides				
	Bailey				
	Fair Isle				
	Faeroes				
	SE. Iceland				

* Mark gale areas * Connect areas grouped in forecast

COASTAL REPORTS Shipping Bulletin At . . . . GMT/BST	Wind		Weather	Visibili.	Pressure	Trend
	Direc	Force				
Tiree						
Butt of Lewis						
Sumburgh						
Bell Rock						
Dowsing						
Dover						
Royal Sovereign						
Channel L.V.						
Scilly						
Valentia						
Ronaldsway						
Malin Head						
Jersey						

COASTAL REPORTS Inshore Waters At . . . . GMT/BST	Wind		Weather	Visibili.	Pressure	Trend
	Direc	Force				
Boulmer						
Spurn Head						
Walton on the Naze						
St. Catherine's Point						
Land's End						
Mumbles						
Valley						
Blackpool						
Prestwick						
Benbecula						
Stornoway						
Lerwick						
Wick						
Aberdeen						
Leuchars						

Chapter 2

The Shipping Forecast

And now the Shipping Forecast issued by the Met. Office at 23.58 on Tuesday the 4th of March.

There are warnings of gales in Viking, Shannon, Rockall. Malin, Hebrides, Bailey, Fair Isle and Faeroes.

The general Synopsis at 18.00. Low Southeast England 1021, moving slowly East and losing its identity soon. New High developing East Biscay with pressure 1035 by 18.00 on Wednesday. Low North Iceland 970 moving slowly North and deepening 964 by that time.

The Area Forecast for the Next 24.00 Hours

Viking, North Utsire, South Utsire, Forties,
Southerly 6 or 7, occasionally gale 8 in Viking, veering Westerly 4 or 5 later, occasional rain, moderate or good.

Cromarty, Forth, Tyne,
Southerly veering Northwesterly later 5 or 6 increasing 7 for a time in Cromarty, occasional rain later, good.

Dogger Fisher,
Southeasterly 4 veering Southwesterly 5 or 6, occasional rain, moderate or good.

German Bight, Humber,
Southeasterly veering Southwesterly 4 or 5, occasional rain, moderate with fog patches.

Thames, Dover, Wight,
Southwesterly temporarily veering Northwesterly in Wight at first 4 occasionally 5, drizzle at first, moderate with fog patches, becoming good for a time.

Portland, Plymouth,
West backing Southwest 4 or 5 occasionally 6 at first veering Northwesterly later, occasional rain, moderate or good becoming poor for a time.

Biscay, Finisterre,
Mainly Southwesterly 4 occasionally 5 in Northwest Finisterre, occasional rain, moderate with fog patches.

Trafalgar,
Mainly Northeasterly 3 or 4, fair, moderate or good.

West Sole,
Southwesterly veering Nortwesterly 5 or 6 becoming variable 3 later, occasional rain, moderate becoming good.

East Sole, Lundy, Fastnet, Irish Sea,
Southwesterly 5 increasing 6 or 7 veering Northwesterly 4 or 5 later, occasional rain, good, becoming moderate or poor for a time.

Shannon,
Westerly 5 or 6 but Southerly 7 or gale 8 in East at first, becoming variable 3 or 4 later, rain at first, moderate or good.

Rockall,
Westerly 5 to 7 but Southerly gale 8 or severe gale 9 in East at first, rain then showers. moderate or poor. becoming good.

Malin, Hebrides,
Southerly 6 to gale 8 occasionally severe gale 9 in Hebrides at first, veering Westerly 5 or 6, rain then showers, moderate occasionally poor becoming good.

Bailey,
Westerly 6 to gale 8, perhaps severe gale 9 later, showers, moderate or good.

Fair Isle,
Southerly 7 to severe gale 9 veering Westerly 6, rain or showers, moderate or good.

Faeroes,
Southerly gale 8 to storm 10 veering Southwesterly 5 to 7, rain then showers, moderate becoming good.

Southeast Iceland,
Southwesterly 5 to 7 perhaps gale 8 later, showers, good.

Now the Weather Reports from Coastal Stations for 23.00 GMT on the 4th of March

Tiree: South by East 7, 7 miles, 1014, falling.

Stornoway: South by West 7, 16 miles, 1010, falling.

Lerwick: South 6, 13 miles, 1013, falling.

Fifeness: Southeast by South 5, 5 miles, 1019, falling.

Bridlington: Southwest by South 2, fog, 700 meters, 1021, falling more slowly.

Sandettie Light-Vessel Automatic: South by West 4, 2 miles, 1023, falling slowly.

Greenwich Light-Vessel Automatic: Southwest by South 4, 5 miles, 1026, rising slowly.

Jersey: West 4, 11 miles, 1027, rising more slowly.

Channel Light-Vessel Automatic: West by North 6, 1025, rising slowly.

Scilly Automatic: Southwest 3, 15 miles, 1026, falling slowly.

Valentia: South by West 4, 16 miles, 1020, falling.

Ronaldsway: Southwest by South 3, 7 miles, 1021, falling slowly.

Malinhead: South 5, 16 miles, 1015, falling.

Now here is,

The Weather Forecast for the Inshore Waters of Great Britain and Northern Ireland until 18.00 on Wednesday the 5th of March

Shallow low Southeast England, moving slowly East and filling, marked cold front lying Northeast to Southwest, moving East across Scotland and Northern Ireland and expected to lie from Berwick upon Tweed to Cardigan Bay by 18-00.

From Berwick upon Tweed to Flamborough Head. Wind Southerly 3 increasing 4 or 5 occasionally, occasional rain or drizzle, visibility moderate, occasionally poor.

From Flamborough Head to North Foreland: Wind Southerly 3, veering Southwesterly 4 or 5, occasional drizzle,visibility moderate with fog patches at first.

From North Foreland to the Lizard Península: Wind Westerly backing Southwesterly 4 or 5, occasional drizzle, visibility moderate occasionally poor.

From the Lizard Península to Cardigan Bay: Wind Southwesterly 4 increasing 5 or 6. occasional drizzle later, visibility good becoming moderate or poor.

From Cardigan Bay to Islay including Carlingford Lough to Lough Foyle: Wind Southwesterly veering Northwesterly later 4 increasing 5 to 7 for a time, occasional rain or drizzle clearing from Northwest later, visibility moderate or poor becoming good.

From Islay to Wick including the waters around Orkney and Shetland: Wind Southwesterly 6 to gale 8 locally severe gale 9 around the Western and Northern Isles veering Westerly 4 or 5, rain then showers, visibility moderate becoming good.

and finally,

From Wick to Berwick upon Tweed. Wind Southerly veering Northwesterly later 5 increasing 6 or 7 for a time, rain then showers, visibility good becoming moderate for a time.

And there is the Remainder of the Weather Reports from Coastal Stations for 23.00 GMT on the 4th of March

Boulmer: South by West 3, mist, 2 miles, 1020, falling.

Bridlington: Southwest by South 2, fog, 700 metres, 1021, falling more slowly.

Sheerness: Southeast by South 1, 4 miles.

St. Catherine´s Point: South Southwest 2, fog, 600 meters, 1023, falling slowly.

Scilly Automatic: Southwest 3, 15 miles, 1026, falling slowly.

Milford Haven: West Southwest 2, 8 miles, 1024, now falling.

Averporth: Southwest by West 3, mist, 3 miles, 1024, now falling.

Valley: Southwest by South 3, intermittent slight drizzle, 2 miles, 1022, falling slowly.

Liverpool Crossby: South by East 3, 1022, falling more slowly.

Ronaldsway: Southwest by South 3, 7 miles, 1021, falling slowly.

Killough: Southwest 3, 16 miles.

Larne: South by West 3, 7 miles.

Mackrihanish: Southeast by South 3, 2 miles, 1018, falling.

Greenock: Continuous slight drizzle, 4 miles, 1019, fallling slowly.

Stornoway: South by West 7, 16 miles, 1010, falling.

Lerwick: South 6, 13 miles, 1013, falling.

Wick: South Southeast 5, 1014, falling.

Aberdeen: Southeast by South 4, haze, 4 miles, 1017, falling.

And finally,

Leuchars: South by East 2, 11 miles, 1018, falling.

And that is the shipping bulletin.

EXERCISES

A. **Blank Filling**

After listening to the weather forecast complete the empty spaces with single words from the passage.

And now the . . . . issued by the Met. Office at . . . . . on Tuesday the . . . .

There are . . . . in Viking, Shannon, ..., Malin, ..., Bailey, Fair Isle and . . . .

The general Synopsis at 18.00 . . . ., 1021, moving slowly . . . . and . . . . its identity soon. New . . . . developing East Biscay with pressure . . . . by . . . . on Wedenesday. . . . . 970 moving slowly North and deepening 964 by that time.

The Area Forecast for the Next 24.00 Hours

Viking, ..., South Utsire, ... Southerly . . . ., occasionally gale . . . ., veering Westerly 4 or 5 later, ocassinal rain, ... or good.

Chromarty, Forth, Tyne,
Southerly . . . . Northwesterly later 5 or 6 increasing . . . . in Chromarty, ocassional . . . ., good.

Dogger, Fisher,
. . . ., occasional rain, moderate or good.

German Bight, ...,
Southeasterly . . . . 4 or 5, occasional rain, moderate with . . . . s.

B. True or False Statements

After carefully listening to the weather forecast, study the following sentences and state wether they are true or false according to the information in the text.

	T	F
1. This shipping forecast has been issued by the Met. Office.	☐	☐
2. Ocassional gale force winds can be expected in Forties.	☐	☐
3. Biscay and Finisterre can expect a good visibility.	☐	☐
4. The forecast for Shannon assumes a rapid weather deterioration.	☐	☐
5. An improvement in the visbility for the Rockall area can be expected.	☐	☐
6. Northern sea areas are experiencing severe weather conditions.	☐	☐

C. Matching Words

Match the words under list A with the words under list B. List B has some extra items.

A	B
1. visibility poor	a) same barometric pressure.
2. occasional	b) extending far down.
3. bright	c) sea area in which wind blows in the same direction.
4. spells	d) a low pressure system.
5. patchy fog	e) becoming greater.
6. improving	f) short periods of sun bright.
7. increasing	g) from time to time.
8. deepening	h) visibility less than 2 n. miles.
9. low	i) discontinuous fog.
10. high	j) a high pressure system.
11. isobar	k) sunny.
12. fetch	l) becoming better.

D. Weather Report Form Filling

Fill in the weather information for the sea area of Biscay and Sole, on the next page form.

R. MET.SOC. / R.Y.A. METMAP (Revised Feb 1986)

GENERAL SYPNOSIS at . . . . GMT/BST . . . .

Gale	SEA AREA FORECAST		Wind	Weather	Visibility
	Viking				
	N. Utsire				
	S. Utsire				
	Forties				
	Cromarty				
	Forth				
	Tyne				
	Dogger				
	Fisher				
	German Bight				
	Humber				
	Thames				
	Dover				
	Wight				
	Portland				
	Plymouth				
	Biscay				
	Finisterre				
	Sole				
	Lundy				
	Fastnet				
	Irish Sea				
	Shannon				
	Rockall				
	Malin				
	Hebrides				
	Bailey				
	Fair Isle				
	Faeroes				
	SE. Iceland				

* Mark gale areas * Connect areas grouped in forecast

COASTAL REPORTS Shipping Bulletin At . . . . GMT/BST	Wind		Weather	Visibili.	Pressure	Trend
	Direc	Force				
Tiree						
Butt of Lewis						
Sumburgh						
Bell Rock						
Dowsing						
Dover						
Royal Sovereign						
Channel L.V.						
Scilly						
Valentia						
Ronaldsway						
Malin Head						
Jersey						

COASTAL REPORTS Inshore Waters At . . . . GMT/BST	Wind		Weather	Visibili.	Pressure	Trend
	Direc	Force				
Boulmer						
Spurn Head						
Walton on the Naze						
St. Catherine's Point						
Land's End						
Mumbles						
Valley						
Blackpool						
Prestwick						
Benbecula						
Stornoway						
Lerwick						
Wick						
Aberdeen						
Leuchars						

Chapter 3

The Interview

Come rain or shine, she checks at 08-45 in the morning, makes a record five times a day and finishes at 9 o'clock in the evening.

Fran Lockier is one of the members of amateur weather-observers all around the country, who is sending reports by computer to the Met. Office.

Claudia Hammond talked to the BBC weather-man here in Glasgow and visited Fran in Portland Bill in Dorset, where she runs a bed and breakfast from the light -house.

It's 08:45 and I am just going out to see the weather for the Met. Office.

I start off by walking along the path and climbing steps to see what visibility I've got. This morning it´s pretty terrible, it´s about 3 kilometers, and not very far at all, it's very overcast and the cloud is very low, I would think, I have 8/8 stratus probably above a thousand feet. I have to put a weather coding in, and of those there are hundred different alternatives, and it starts off with the cloud being more or less, the visibility being more or less, and it goes through all the various forms of precipitation,from fog to rain, to drizzle, to snow, to hail...

Shipping Forecast

It's 5 to 2, and now the Shipping Forecast issued by the Met. Office at 13-05 on Monday the 22nd of January.

"There are warnings of gales in Viking, South Utsire, Forties, Chromarty, Dogger, Fisher, German Bight".

I measure the rain fall just as I grade it, it's a litle thing I pour it into, and read off how much there is. On this particular morning we've got 3 milimeters not very much, but a measurable amount. And the thermometers of course are the other things, that give you the maximun and minimum temperatures.

It has to be a statutory height above the ground and in a fairly exposed position, so that obviously it gets the worst and the best of the weather.

We've always relied heavily on amateur weather observers, just to fill in the holes in the network. It would be prohibitively expensive to have a network of professional observers,ah, every fifty kilometers or so along the country. And in fact whith a wonderful piece dividend,so areas of observing stations are closing all over the country, and our network is becoming even more sparse, so that we're becoming to rely more and more on those decent professionals I mean that, amateur observers.

...You never have a lie-in. I do occasionally go out because now it's semi-automatic, it's not so vital if I miss an observation, because they still get the automatic data, which is the wind speed and direction, and the temperatures, the humidity, the barometric pressure,all that is done automatically, so they´ve still got all that, if I happen to go out and stay out too long.

We have some younger ones as well, but we do need a constant supply of new young observers. The difficulty is of course that they have to be a sort of more or less sort of stuck in one place for thirty years, but this often does happen with some professionals such as people who look after the Post Office, they make wonderful observers.

We used to have a sunshine recorder on there, and I'll show you the sunshine recorder, that's a glass orb, that is set in a frame and a card fixed behind the glass orb. And the sun just burns through the orb and burns a trace in the paper-card behind, and you measure the lenght of the trace, now that orb use to be on top of the light-house.

We've now got it situated somewhere a little bit more convenient for me, so I don't have to traipse all the way up to the top of the tower.

So the top of the tower is a sunlight observatory that's used by B & B guests.

Shipping Forecast

Portland, Plymouth, easterly 6 to gale 8, veering southeasterly 4, rain, moderate or good.

I frequently have to leave the breakfast, to come out and do the weather, because quarter to nine obviously is the time you are serving breakfast, isn't it. So you come out and you do the weather and go back and you say sorry I'm a bit late, but you know, I was doing the weather. Oh, what it is going to be today?, everybody always wants to know, you know, so you got to stick your neck out a little bit here and there. What if you are ill, is there someone else helping? I drag myself out and feel absolutly wretched and do as quickly as I can and get back in bed. I think, I´ve only missed ever about once trough being ill. It's not so bad now, but when I used to have to hold a hand-held anemometer, I still have to go up half a dozen steps, and hold it in the teeth of the wind, and sometimes if it's blowing, you know, anything up to hundred miles an hour, I mean, it happens, and you are standing there, you are shaking and trying to hold on and hold this anemometer, and then, from that, you have to add a third on top of what it read, because it was only considered accurate for that level.

Have you ever forgotten to do it? Yes, a couple of misses I had, Oh! sometimes you remember, oh the weather and you go tearing out and rushing back, a few seconds late, but I really hate myself. I put a little note in the margin saying late. A black mark

Fran LOCKIER

EXERCISES

A. The Missing Letters

Add **u, y, o, ff, w, light, b, y, hi, a, house, e, th, breakfast, u, zz, a, a, m, a,** *to these words in the right places. All the words are in the text.*

s. . . n . .	h. . il
wea. . . . er	g . . les
bed and	te . . perature
p . . th	d . .ta
light	s . . ppl . .
visi . . ilit . .	P . .st O. . . . ice
strat . . s	to . . er
dri. . . . le	sun . . . .

B. True or False Statements

After listening to the lesson, state whether the sentences below are true or false according to the information in the passage.

		T	F
1.	She registers the weather conditions 3 times a day.	☐	☐
2.	One of the items to be checked is visibility.	☐	☐
3.	Gale warnings have been issued for Viking.	☐	☐
4.	Most of the observations are carried out by profesional observers.	☐	☐
5.	The data is recorded manually.	☐	☐
6.	People living always in the same place would make good observers.	☐	☐
7.	Portland and Plymouth can expect a weather improvement later.	☐	☐
8.	The wind in Portland is changing direction clock-wise.	☐	☐
9.	An anemometer is an instrument for measuring wind speed.	☐	☐
10.	She gets always in time fo her readings.	☐	☐

C. **Vocabulary**

Clouds

The names of the clouds are composed of various combinations of the basic words, all from Latin:

Alto, meaning "high"
Cirrus, meaning "curl"
Cumulus, meaning "an accumulation"
Nimbus, meaning "rainy cloud"
Stratus, meaning "layers"

The 3 principal cloud divisions are:

High Clouds, lower level above 20,000 feet = 6.000 meters

Cirrus
Cirrocumulus
Cirrostratus

Midle Clouds, mean level between 6,500 and 20,000 feet = 1,950 and 6.000 meters

Altocumulus
Altostratus

Low Clouds, mean lower level less than 6,500 feet = 1,950 meters

Stratocumulus
Stratus
Nimbostratus
Cumulus
Cumulonimbus

CLOUDS

Altocomulus

Cirrocumulus

Cirrus/Cirrostratus

Cirrus

Cirrus

Stratocumulus

Altocumulus

Cirrocumulus

Altostratus

Beginnings of Cumulus

Cirrostratus

Sea Fog

Swelling Cumulus

Cumulus of Fair Weather

Cumulus Congestus

Cumulusnimbus

Cumulus of Fair Weather

Find the cloud names which match the definitions given below.

1. High cloud, of delicate and fibrous appearance, generally white and silky, composed by ice cristals, appears in varied forms such as isolated tufts, long thin lines across the sky.
2. High cloud, composed of ice cristals, generally associated with fair weather, one form of them is popularly known as "mackerel sky" because the pattern resembles the scales on the back of a mackerel. They may turn gray and appear hard before thickening.
3. Middle cloud, of grayish or bluish appearance, fibrous veil or sheet. The sun or moon, when seen trough these clouds, appears as if it were shining through a ground glass, with a corona around it. If these clouds thicken and lower, or if low, rain clouds nimbostratus can form below them, continuous rain or snow may be expected.
4. Low cloud, dense with vertical development, appear in small patches and never cover the whole sky, dome-shaped, with protuberances extending above the dome. It has an horizontal base.
5. Low cloud, with great vertical development, rising in mountainous towers to great heights, often spreads out in the form of an anvil. It often produces showers, rain, hail, or snow, frequently accompanied by thunder.

1. □□□□□□
2. □□□□□□□□□□□□
3. □□□□□□□□□□□
4. □□□□□□□
5. □□□□□□□□□□□□

Chapter 4

The Shipping Forecast

For Monday the 4th. of March.

This is Radio 4, it's now 5 to 2, time for the Shipping Forecast issued by the Met. Office at 13.05 today, Monday the 4th of March.

The General Synopsis today at 06.00. High 150' West of Rockall, 1035, drifting slowly South,with little change.

The Area Forecast for the Next 24 Hours

Viking, North Utsire, South Utsire, Forties,
Northerly 5 or 6, occasionally 7 at first, occasional drizzle, moderate or good.

Cromarty,
Northerly 4 or 5, occasionally 6 at first, mainly fair, moderate or good.

Forth, Tyne,
Northwesterly 3 or 4, occasionally 5, mainly fair, moderate or good.

Dogger,
Northerly 5 or 6, mainly fair, moderate or good.

Fisher,
Northerly 5 or 6, decreasing 3 or 4, but variable 4 in East at first, mainly fair, moderate or good.

German Bight,
Northerly 4 or 5, decreasing 3 or 4, but variable 3 in East at first, occasional drizzle, moderate or good, occasionally poor.

Humber,
Northerly 4 or 5 occasionally 6 at first, occasional drizzle, moderate or good.

Thames, Dover,
Northerly 4 or 5 occasionally 6 at first, occasional drizzle, moderate occasionally poor.

Wight, Portland, Plymouth,
North or Northeast 3 or 4, occasionally 5, mainly fair, moderate or good.

Biscay,
Northeasterly 4 or 5, occasionally 3 in East, mainly fair, moderate or good.

Finisterre,
Northeasterly 5 or 6, occasionally 7 near Cape Finisterre, fair, good.

Sole,
Northeasterly 4 or 5, occasionally 6, fair, good.

Lundy, Fastnet,
North or Northeast 3 or 4, occasionally 5, occasional drizzle, moderate or good.

Irish Sea,
North or Northwest 3 or 4, occasionally 5, occasional drizzle, moderate or good.

Shannon,
North or Northeast 3 or 4, mainly fair, moderate or good.

Rockall, Malin,
North or Northwest 3 or 4, mainly fair, moderate or good.

Hebrides,
North westerly 3 or 4, occcasionally 5, mainly fair, moderate or good.

Bailey,
West or Northwest 4 or 5, fair, good.

Fair Isle,
Northwesterly 5 or 6, occasional rain, moderate or good.
Faeroes,
West or Northwest 4, increasing 5 or 6, rain, moderate or good.
and
South-East Iceland,
West or Southwest 5 or 6, occasionally 7, rain, moderate or poor becoming good.

And Now,
Weather Reports from Coastal Stations for 12.00 GMT.

Tiree: North 4, 22 miles, 1029, now rising
Stornoway: Northwest 2, 16 miles, 1030, rising more slowly.
Sumburgh: North, Northwest 5, recent drizzlle, 13 miles, 1025, falling slowly.
Fifeness: Northwest by West 3, 7 miles, 1027, now falling.
Bridlington: Northwest 4, 8 miles, 1025, falling slowly.
Dover: North -Northeast 5, mist, 4 miles, 1023, rising slowly
Greenwich Light-Vessel Automatic: North 4, more than 27 miles, 1024, steady.
Jersey: North by West 2, intermittent slight rain, 6 miles, 1025, falling slowly.
Channel Light-Vessel Automatic: North 4, 5 miles, 1026, rising slowly.
Scilly Automatic: North Northeast 3, 9 miles, 1028, rising slowly.
Valentia: North 3, 7 miles, 1031, rising slowly.
Ronaldsway: Northwest by North 3, 9 miles, 1028, rising slowly
and finally,
Malin Head: North 4, 24 miles, 1030, falling more slowly.
and that's the end of the shipping forecast.

EXERCISES

A. Dialogue

Write a dialogue between a sailor and the control tower. These words and letters, ***o, ast, wrong, about, sea, set off, situation, drastically, sky, happening, threatening, sense, coastguards, m, ss, called, a, e,*** *will help you.*

Control What! What are you talking . . . . ?
Sailor Look, in the last few minutes the . . . . state has changed . . . .
Control But that's i. . po. . . . ible. Since you set off the sea state hasn't changed.
Sailor Well, since I last . . . . you, the w. .v. .s are 5 meters high.
Control But we checked the weather f. . rec . . . . . before you set off.
Sailor Well, there's something . . . . wit it. And the sky has turned yellow and . . . .
Control But that doesn't make . . . . Since you . . . . the weather here is good with a clear . . . .
Sailor I don't know what's . . . . I have never experienced a . . . . like this.
Control I'll contact the . . . .

B. **Matching Words**

Match the words under list A with the words under list B. List B has some extra items.

A	B
1. Season	a) continuous rain more common in spring.
2. Sudden downpour	b) type of rain more common in winter.
3. Drizzle and falls	c) very heavy rain from a cloud.
4. Steady driving rain	d) sudden gust of wind.
5. Heatwave	e) type of rain more common in summer.
6. Cloudbursts	f) one or four divisions of year.
7. Rainfall	g) amount of fallen water measured and recorded.
8. Squall	h) an access of excessive heat in the atmosphere.

Chapter 5

Weather Forecast

This is the roll in the roast to the West of he British Isle, so our weather changes are going to be continuously very slow moving, but just look as we look ahead things are in fact going to get colder, as we go towards the week-end. Let's come back to Today and start with the whole of England and Wales. For most of us is going to be a cloudy afternoon, with many areas staying dry. The cloud cover's still thick enough to bring some patchy light rain and drizzle to parts of East Anglia, and the central Severn and eastern regions of England.

We also may see some brief spells over parts of East Anglia and southeast of England at times as well, temperatures around 7 to 9 celsius this afternoon.

Cool over the eastern coastal counties and a light northerly breeze.

And then tonight little changes, patchy, light rain or drizzle, again affecting many eastern regions of England, and pushing through into the eastern Midlands, elsewhere mostly dry, and under clear skies quite cool as the temperatures fall down about 2 to 4 celsius in the western areas.

Now, moving to Northern Ireland, where we head to a generally cloudy afternoon, but a mainly dry afternoon, we may just see the odd spot or two of rain in one or two coastal areas, the wind is light and northerly.

And the top temperatures reaching around 8 degrees likely, and that's 46 Farenheit.

Overnight it´s going to stay dry, with some gaps developing in the cloud, and that should allow temperatures to fall back to around, about 3 degrees.

And finally to Scotland, much of Scotland is going to have a dry afternoon with the cloud breaking to allow some bright or sunny spells.

The best of the sunshine will probably be persisting over the southern and southwestern most regions of Scotland.

And elsewhere, we'll see some patchy precipitations persisting over the Northern Isles.

Temperatures this afternoon reaching around to 9 or 10 celsius in the sunnier locations. And, then tonight, rather more cloud over the northern regions of Scotland, bringing a scattering of light showers in some exposed areas.

Elsewhere staying dry with the clear skies allowing frost and fog to form, in for example such areas as the Central Lowlands as temperatures fall back to around minus 2 or minus 3 celsius.

Now looking ahead to Wednesday and Thursday, the high pressure very much stays in control, on Wedenesday it means further light precipitation to start the day over eastern counties of England. This will tend to die away during the morning and then with the prospect of some brighter skies nudging in from the west as we go through the day.

Away from the eastern most counties basically another dry day, quite a lot of cloud around but also some sunny intervals, as well.

On Thursday we'll begin to see a bit of a change as patchy rain and drizzle, spreads from the southeast over much of England and Wales throughout the day.

That's the forecast.

EXERCISES

A. **Weather Forecast**

This is the weather forecast for Great Britain. Answer these questions by choosing the best alternative (A, B, C, or D). Think carefully before you make your choice.

1. Today England and Wales can expect
   A. thunderstorms.
   B. continuous rain.
   C. cloudy skies.
   D. high winds.

2. This afternoon East Anglia can expect
   A. sunshine.
   B. slight frost.
   C. drizzle.
   D. increasingly strong winds.

3. The eastern coastal counties can expect
   A. snow showers.
   B. strong winds.
   C. increasing cold.
   D. mild temperatures.

4. The eastern Midlands can expect
   A. light rain or drizzle.
   B. occasional rain.
   C. a dry evening.
   D. widespread fog.

5. In the afternoon North Ireland can expect
   A. a rainy day.
   B. temperatures below freezing point.
   C. a dry afternoon.
   D. sunny spells.

B. **Multiple Choice**

Underneath each sentence there are four words. Consider which of them will be suitable, so you must look at each alternative very carefully.

1. There is a . . . . channel with litle water.
   A Deep **B** Shallow **C** Twisted **D** Small
2. The Met.Office is planning . . . ., expecting to be storing data by 2005.
   A Ahead **B** Though **C** Freely **D** To go public
3. He at last . . . . his ambition of sailing across the Atlantic.
   A Effected **B** Achieved **C** Performed **D** Completed
4. A light to . . . . easterly wind.
   A Strong **B** Thundery **C** Moderate **D** Breeze
5. Slight to . . . . seas.
   A Large **B** Big **C** Strong **D** Moderate
6. Low B will . . . . thus diminishing its pressure.
   A Go up **B** Decrease **C** Deepen **D** Improve
7. Low A will . . . . thus increasing its pressure.
   A Go up **B** Fill **C** Grow up **D** Sweep

Chapter 6

The Shipping Forecast

Now, it's 5 to 2, the Shipping Forecast issued by the Met. Office at 13.05. The general synopsis at 06-00.

High 100 miles west of Rockall 1034, expected Malin 1034 by 06.00 tomorrow.

The Area Forecast for the Next 24 Hours

Viking, North and South Utsire, Forties,
Northwesterly veering Northerly 4 or 5, occasionally 6, showers, moderate or good.

Cromarty,
Northwesterly veering Northerly 4, occasionally 5, mainly fair, moderate or good.

Forth, Tyne,
Northwesterly 3 or 4, occasionally 5, mainly fair, moderate or good.

Dogger,
North or Northwest 4 or 5, mainly fair, moderate or good.

Fisher, German Bight,
Northwesterly 3 or 4, but 5 in West, occasional rain or drizzle, moderate or good but fog patches in German Bight at first.

Humber,
Northerly 4 or 5, occasional rain or drizzle, moderate or good.

Thames, Dover,
North or Northwest 3 or 4, occasionally 5, occasional rain or drizzle, moderate or good.

Wight,
North or Northeast 3 or 4, fair, good.

Portland, Plymouth,
Northeasterly 3 or 4, fair good.

Biscay,
Northeasterly 4 or 5 occasionally 6 in South, fair, moderate or good.

Finisterre,
Northeasterly 4 or 5 occasionally 6 but 7 at times, near Cape Finisterre, mainly fair, mainly good.

Sole,
Northeasterly veering Easterly 3 or 4, fair, good.

Lundy, Fastnet, Irish Sea,
North or Northeast 3 or 4, fair, good.

Shannon,
Variable, mainly Northeasterly veering Southeasterly 3 or 4, fair, good.

Rockall,
Variable 3 or less becoming Southeasterly 4, fair, good.

Malin,
Variable, mainly Northerly then Southeasterly 3, occasionally 4, fair, good.

Hebrides,
West or Northwest 4, occasionally 5, then variable 3, occasional drizzle, moderate or good.

Bailey,
West backing Southwest 4 or 5 occasionally 6, occcasional rain or drizzle, good becoming moderate or poor.

Fair Isle,
Northwesterly 4 or 5, decreasing 3, occasional drizzle. moderate or good.

Faeroes,
West or Northwest 4 or 5, occasionally 6, backing Southwesterly 3 or 4, occasional rain or drizzle, moderate or good.

South-East Iceland,
Westerly 4 or 5, backing Southwesterly 6 or 7, perhaps gale 8 later, occasional rain or drizzle, good becoming moderate, occasionally poor.

Now
Weather Reports from Coastal Stations for 12.00 GMT.

Tiree: Northwest 3, recent showers, 11 miles, 1031, rising slowly

Stornoway: West 4, 32 miles, 1029, now rising.

Sumburgh: West Northwest 4, 16 miles, 1023, falling slowly.

Fifeness: South Southwest 3, haze, 4 miles, 1029, falling slowly.

Bridlington: North 3, 11 miles, 1029, rising slowly.

Dover: North by East 4, 11 miles, 1027, rising slowly.

Greenwich Light-Vessel Automatic: North 4, more than 27 miles, 1029, rising slowly.

Jersey: North by East 3, 11 miles, 1029, now falling.

Channel Light-Vessel Automatic: North by East 3, 5 miles, 1030, rising slowly.

Scilly Automatic: Northeast by North 3, 9 miles, 1030, rising slowly.

Valentia: Northeast 1, 24 miles, 1032, now rising.

Ronaldsway: West Northwest 3, 16 miles, 1031, rising slowly.

and

Malin Head: North Northwest 3, precipitation within sight, 22 miles, 1032, rising slowly.

EXERCISES

A. Matching Words

Match the words under list A with the meanings given under list B.

A	B
1. longitude	a) rapid movement of air in circles.
2. ripple	b) pattern in which the air flows.
3. windshock	c) sudden burst of wind.
4. rain	d) facing the wind.
5. drift	e) very small slow wave.
6. hazy	f) cone-shaped bag on a mast to show the direction of the wind.
7. hail	g) moisture falling in drops from clouds.
8. breeze	h) frozen vapour falling in pellets.
9. spin	i) dense watery vapour in lower atmosphere.
10. gust	j) misty.
11. eddy	k) carried away by the sea currents or wind.
12. wreckage	l) loud noise accompanying lightning.
13. sleet	m) gentle wind.
14. fog	n) broken remains, especially of a ship.
15. upwind	o) angular distance east or west from Greenwich.
16. flow pattern	p) round rapidly.
17. thunder	q) rain and snow or hail falling together.
18. storm	r) condensed water vapour floating in air.
19. cloud	s) flat floating structure, life-raft.
20. raft	t) violent wind or disturbance of atmosphere.

B. Weather Report Form Filling

Fill in the weather report form provided on the next page, for the following adjacent areas Hebrides, Bailey, Fair Isle, Faeroes and Southeast Iceland.

R. MET.SOC. / R.Y.A. METMAP (Revised Feb 1986)

GENERAL SYPNOSIS at . . . . GMT/BST . . . .

Gale	SEA AREA FORECAST		Wind	Weather	Visibility
	Viking				
	N. Utsire				
	S. Utsire				
	Forties				
	Cromarty				
	Forth				
	Tyne				
	Dogger				
	Fisher				
	German Bight				
	Humber				
	Thames				
	Dover				
	Wight				
	Portland				
	Plymouth				
	Biscay				
	Finisterre				
	Sole				
	Lundy				
	Fastnet				
	Irish Sea				
	Shannon				
	Rockall				
	Malin				
	Hebrides				
	Bailey				
	Fair Isle				
	Faeroes				
	SE. Iceland				

* Mark gale areas * Connect areas grouped in forecast

COASTAL REPORTS Shipping Bulletin At . . . . GMT/BST	Wind		Weather	Visibili.	Pressure	Trend
	Direc	Force				
Tiree						
Butt of Lewis						
Sumburgh						
Bell Rock						
Dowsing						
Dover						
Royal Sovereign						
Channel L.V.						
Scilly						
Valentia						
Ronaldsway						
Malin Head						
Jersey						

COASTAL REPORTS Inshore Waters At . . . . GMT/BST	Wind		Weather	Visibili.	Pressure	Trend
	Direc	Force				
Boulmer						
Spurn Head						
Walton on the Naze						
St. Catherine's Point						
Land's End						
Mumbles						
Valley						
Blackpool						
Prestwick						
Benbecula						
Stornoway						
Lerwick						
Wick						
Aberdeen						
Leuchars						

C. **Vocabulary**

Read the definitions provided, and find the corresponding technical word.

1. Wind experienced by an observer aboard a vessel proceeding through still air, equal to the speed of the vessel.
2. Set designed for measuring the wind speed.
3. Scale at wich pure water freezes at 32° and boils at 212°.
4. The lowest possible temperature.
5. Temperature at which the moisture deposits upon natural objects.
6. Fine dust or salt particles in the air suficiente to reduce visibility.
7. Set designed for measuring the relative humidity and dew point.
8. The belt of low pressures at the surface near the equator at about latitudes 30° to 35°.
9. Winds blowing at the surface from the belts of high pressure toward the equatorial belts of low pressure.
10. Apparent force exerted by the rotation of the Earth.

1. □□□□□□□□-□□□□
2. □□□□□□□□□□
3. □□□□□□□□□
4. □□□□□□□□-□□□□
5. □□□□□□□□
6. □□□□
7. □□□□□□□□□□
8. □□□□□□□□
9. □□□□□-□□□□□
10. □□□□□□□□

Chapter 7

The Shipping Forecast

And now, the Shipping Forecast issued by the Met. Office at 23.58 on Monday the 15th of July.

The General Synopsis at 19-00, High, Hebrides 1037, expected Fair Isle 1036 by 19.00 Tuesday.

New High developing Dogger 1037 by same time. Low Spain 1014 slow moving with little change.

The Area Forecast for the Next 24 Hours

Viking,
Northwesterly 4 or 5, occasionally 6 at first, showers dying out, mainly good.

North Utsire, South Utsire,
Northwesterly 5 or 6, occasionally 7 at first, showers, good.

Forties,
Northwesterly 4 or 5, becoming variable 3 in West, mainly fair, good.

Crormarty, Forth, Tyne,
Variable 3 or 4, fair, mainly good.

Dogger,
Northerly 4, becoming variable 3, mainly fair, good.

Fisher, German Bight,
Northwesterly 5 or 6, occasionally 7 at first in Fisher, showers, good.

Humber,
North veering Northeast 4 or 5, mainly fair, good.
Thames, Dover,
Northeasterly 4 or 5, increasing 6 or 7 at times, fair, mainly good.
Wight, Portland, Plymouth,
Northeasterly 4 or 5, occasionally 6, fair, moderate or good but poor in South Plymouth at first.
Biscay,
Northeasterly 3 or 4, increasing 5 in North, fair, moderate or good but poor in North at first.
Trafalgar,
Mainly Northwesterly 3 or 4, but Northeasterly 5 or 6 in far Southeast at times, mainly fair, moderate or good.
South-Finisterre,
Northeasterly becoming variable 3 or 4, mainly fair, moderate or good.
North-Finisterre, Sole,
Northeast veering East 3 or 4 occasionally 5, occasional drizzle in West, moderate with fog patches becoming good in East.
Lundy, Fastnet,
Northeast veering East 4 occasionally 5, fair, mainly good.
Irish Sea,
Northeast veering East 3 or 4, fair, good.
Shannon,
East veering Southeast 3 or 4, increasing 5 in South, mainly fair, good.
Rockall,
Variable becoming Southeasterly 3 or 4, fair, mainly good.
Malin,
Northerly veering Southeasterly 3 or 4, fair, good.
Hebrides,
Variable 3 or 4, fair, mainly good.
Bailey,
South or Southwest 3 or 4, occasionally 5 in North, mainly fair, moderate or good.

Fair Isle,
West or Northwest 3 or 4, occasionally 5 in North, fair, mainly good.

Faeroes,
West or Southwest 3 or 4, occasionally 5 in North, mainly fair, good.

and

Southeast Iceland,
Westerly 4 or 5, occasional drizzle later, good becoming moderate or poor.

And now,

The Weather Reports from Coastal Stations for 23.00 B.S.T. Yesterday

Tiree: North by West 2, more than 38 miles, 1036, rising slowly

Stornoway: Calm. shallow fog, 35 miles, 1037, rising more slowly.

Lerwick: West by North 4, 16 miles, 1035, now falling.

Fifeness: Calm, 12 miles, 1038, rising slowly.

Bridlington: North 3, 11 miles, 1036, rising slowly.

Sandettie Light-Vessel Automatic: Northeast 5, more than 27 miles, 1032, rising slowly.

Greenwich Light-Vessel Automatic: East 6, 11 miles, 1031, rising slowly.

Jersey: Northeast 5, 7 miles, 1028, rising slowly.

Channel Light-Vessel Automatic: Northeast by East 4, 5 miles, 1029.

Scilly Automatic: Northeast 3, 1029, rising slowly.

Valentia: Southeast by South 1, 32 miles, 1032, rising slowly.

Ronaldsway: Northeast by East 3, 27 miles, 1035, rising slowly.

and,

Malin Head: Northeast 3, more than 38 miles, 1036, rising more slowly.

And now here is,

The Weather Forecast for the Inshore Waters of Great Britain and Northern Ireland. Until 18-00 hours today, Tuesday the 16th of July

An Anticyclone to the Northwest of Scotland, will be slow moving, while another forms over the North Sea.

From Berwick Upon Tweed to Flamborough Head: Wind, variable 2 or 3, fair, visibility mainly good.

From Flamborough Head to Lowestoft: Wind, Northeast veering East 3 or 4, fair, visibility mainly good.

From Lowestoft to North Foreland: Wind, Northeasterly 3 or 4, increasing 5 or 6, fair, visibility good.

From North Foreland to Beachy Head: Wind, Northeasterly 5, increasing 6 or 7 at times, fair, visibility mainly good.

From Beachy Head to Lands End: Wind Northeast veering East 4 or 5 increasing 6 around headlands, fair, visibility moderate or good.

From Lands End to St. Davis' Head: Wind, Easterly 3 or 4, occasionally 5, fair, visibility mainly good.

From St. Davis' Head to Skye, including Carlingford Lough to Lough Foyle: Wind variable, mainly Northerly becoming Southeasterly 3 or 4, fair, visibility good.

and finally,

From Skye to Berwick upon Tweed including the waters around Orkney and Shetland: Wind, variable 3 or 4, but Westerly 4 or 5 around Shetland at first, mainly fair, visibility good.

And now some further Weather Reports from Coastal Stations at 23.00 B.S.T. Yesterday

Boulmer: Northwest 1, 22 miles, 1037, rising slowly.

Bridlington: North 3, 11 miles, 1036, rising slowly.

Sheerness: At 22-00 BST, Northeast by East 6, 19 miles.

St. Catherine' s Point: East 4, 16 miles, 1031, rising.

Scilly Automatic: Northeast 3, 1029, rising slowly.

Milford Haven: Calm, 1031, rising slowly.

Aberporth: Calm, 19 miles, 1032, rising slowly.

Valley: Northeast 3, 22 miles, 1033, now falling.

Liverpool Crossby: East by North 3, 1035, rising.

Ronaldsway: Northeast by East 3, 27 miles, 1035, rising slowly.

Machrihanish: Calm, 9 miles, 1035, rising slowly.

Stornoway: Calm, shallow fog, 35 miles, 1037, rising more slowly.

Lerwick: West by North 4, 16 miles, 1035, now falling.

Wick-Automatic: West by South 2, 1037, rising slowly.

Aberdeen: Northwest by North 2, more than 38 miles, 1037, rising more slowly.

and finally,

Leuchars: South by East 1, 19 miles, 1037, rising slowly.

EXERCISES

A. Shipping Forecast Terminology

Find single words which correspond to the meanings below.

Winds of at least Beaufort force 8 (34-40 Knots) or gusts reaching 43-51 knots.

_ _ _ _

Winds of force 12 (64 knots or more)

_ _

Expected within 6 hours of time of issue.

_ _ _ _ _ _ _ _ _ _ _ _ _ _

Expected more than 12 hours from time of issue.

_ _ _ _ _ _

Visibility less than 1000 m.

_ _ _

Visibility between 1000 m. and 2 n. miles.

_ _ _ _

Visibility more than 5 n. miles.

_ _ _ _ _ _ _ _

B. **Blank Filling**

After listening to the weather forecast complete the empty spaces with single words from the passage.

The Weather Reports from Coastal Stations for 23.00 B.S.T. Yesterday

Tiree: . . . . 2, more than 38 miles, 1036, rising slowly.

Stornoway: Calm. . . . ., 35miles, 1037, ... more slowly.

Lerwick: West by North 4, 16 miles, 1035, ...

Fifeness: . . . .

Bridlington: North 3, 11 miles, 1036, rising slowly.

Sandettie . . . .: Northeast 5, more than 27 miles, 1032, rising slowly.

Greenwich Light-Vessel Automatic: East 6, 11 miles, 1031, rising slowly.

Jersey: . . . .

Channel Light-Vessel Automatic: . . . ., 5 miles, 1029.

Scilly Automatic: Northeast 3, ..., rising slowly.

Valentia: . . . . 1, 32 miles, 1032, rising slowly.

Ronaldsway: Northeast by East 3, ..., ..., rising slowly.

Chapter 8

The Shipping Forecast

...and now the Shipping Forecast issued by the Met. Office at 23.58 on Monday the 18th of March.

There are warnings of gales in Finisterre, Sole and Southeast Iceland.

The general synopsis at 18-00
Low 150 miles West of Trafalgar, 1002, expected Northwest Sole, 996, by 18-00 on Tuesday.

New High expected 100 miles North of Iceland, 1043, by same time.

The Area Forecast for the Next 24 Hours

Viking, North Utsire,
Southeasterly 3 or 4, mainly fair, moderate or good.

South Utsire, Forties, Cromarty,
Southeasterly 4 or 5, wintry showers, moderate or good.

Forth, Tyne, Dogger,
Easterly veering Southeasterly 3 or 4, occasional rain, moderate or poor.

Fisher,
Southeasterly 5 or 6, decreasing 4, wintry showers, moderate or good.

German Bight,
Southeasterly 4 or 5, decreasing 3, mainly fair, moderate or poor.

Humber, Thames, Dover,
Easterly 3 or 4, mainly fair, moderate or poor with coastal fog patches.

Wight, Portland, Plymouth,
Southeasterly 3 or 4, increasing 5 or 6, showers, moderate or good.

Biscay,
Southeasterly 4 or 5, increasing 6 for a time, rain later, good becoming moderate.

Trafalgar,
Mainly Southwesterly veering Westerly 4 or 5, but southerly 5 or 6 in Northeast at first, rain and showers, moderate or good.

Finisterre,
Southeasterly veering Southwesterly 5 increasing 7 or gale 8 for a time, rain and showers, moderate or good.

Sole,
Southeasterly 4 or 5 increasing 7 or gale 8, rain at times, good becoming moderate.

Lundy, Fasnet,
Southeasterly 3 or 4, increasing 6 or 7, perhaps gale 8 later, showers, moderate or good.

Irish Sea,
Southeasterly 3 or 4, occasionally 5 at first, mainly fair, moderate or poor.

Shannon,
Southeasterly 4, increasing 6 or 7, perhaps gale 8 later, showers then rain, moderate or good.

Rockall, Malin,
Easterly 4 or 5, increasing 6 in South later, occasional rain, moderate or good.

Hebrides,
Easterly 3 or 4, increasing 5 or 6 in North, showers, moderate or good.

Bailey,
Easterly backing Northeasterly 4, increasing 6 or 7, perhaps gale 8 later, rain at times, moderate or good.

Fair Isle,
Southeasterly backing Easterly 4 or 5, rain at times, moderate or good.

Faeroes,
Easterly backing Northeasterly 4, increasing 6 or 7 perhaps gale 8 later, rain at times, moderate or good.

Southeast Iceland,
Easterly backing Northeasterly 4, increasing 6 to gale 8, occasional rain, moderate or good.

now,

The Weather Reports from Coastal Stations at 23-00 G.M.T.

Tiree: Southeast by South 4, haze, 4 miles, 1021, rising more slowly.

Stornoway: Southeast by East 3, 11 miles, 1021, rising slowly.

Sumburgh: Southeast 4, recent rain, 5 miles, 1027, falling slowly.

Fifeness: East by South 4, recent drizzle, 5 miles, 1023, now falling.

Bridlington: East South East 3, haze, 2 miles, 1021, now rising.

Dover: Northeast 3, haze, 1.5 miles, 1019, rising more slowly.

Greenwich Light-Vessel Automatic: East North East 4, 1 mile, 1019, rising slowly.

Jersey: East Northeast 3, 19 miles, 1017, now rising.

Channel Light -Vessel Automatic: Southeast 2, 11 miles, 1017, rising slowly.

Scilly Automatic: Southeast by South 3, 12 miles, 1015, rising slowly.

Valentia: East by South 3, 32 miles, 1013, rising slowly.

Ronaldsway: East by North 5, recent rain, 2 miles, 1019, now falling

Malinhead: East by South 4, mist, 6 miles, 1019, rising slowly.

Now,

The Weather Forecast for the Inshore Waters of Great Britain and Northern Ireland. Until 18.00 today, Tuesday the 19th of March

A Depression will move slowly Northeast towards Southwestern areas.

From Berwick Upon Tweed to Spurn Head: Wind Easterly veering Southeasterly 3 or 4, occasional rain, visibility moderate or poor.

From Spurn Head to Selsey Bill: Wind Easterly 3 or 4, mainly fair, visibility moderate or poor with coastal fog patches.

From Selsey Bill to St. Davis' Head: Wind Southeasterly 3 or 4, increasing 5, occasionally 6 later, mainly fair, visibility moderate or good.

From St. Davis' Head to Mull of Kyntire including Calingford Lough to Lough Foyle: Wind East or Southeast 3 or 4, occasionally 5 at first, mainly fair, visibility moderate or poor.

From Mull of Kyntire to Cape Wrath: Wind Southeasterly 3 or 4, occasional rain, visibility moderate or good.

From Cape Wrath to Wick including the waters around Orkney and Shetland: Wind Southeasterly 4 or 5, mainly fair, visibility moderate or good.

From Wick to Berwick Upon Tweed: Wind Southeasterly 3 or 4, occasionally 5 at first, occasional rain, visibility moderate or poor.

Now,

The Weather Reports from Coastal Stations for 23.00 G.M.T.

Boulmer: East South East 3, continuous light drizzle, 2 miles, 1022, rising slowly.

Bridlington: East South East 3, haze, 2 miles, 1021, now rising.

Walton On The Naze: Northeast 3, haze, 1 mile, 1020, rising slowly.

St. Catherine's Point: East Northeast 3, haze, 3 miles, 1018, rising more slowly.

Scilly Automatic: Southeast by South 3, 12 miles, 1015, rising slowly.

Mumbles: Southeast 3, 7 miles, 1017, rising slowly.

Valley: East 3, haze, 1.5 miles, 1017, rising slowly.

Liverpool Crossby: Southeast by East 3, 1019, rising slowly.

Ronaldsway: East by North 5, recent rain, 2 miles, 1019, now falling.

Larne: East 2, 6 miles.

Machrihanish: East by North 4, haze, 4 miles, 1019, rising slowly.

Greenock: East 4, 7 miles, 1022, rising slowly.

Benbecula: Calm, 1021, rising slowly.

Stornoway: Southeast by East 3, 11 miles, 1021, rising slowly.

Lerwick: Southeast 3, recent showers, 13 miles, 1028, falling more slowly.

Wick: Southeast by East 4, 1025, falling slowly.

Aberdeen: Southeast by East 2, continuous light rain, 2 miles, 1024, falling slowly.

Leuchars: East by South 4, slight drizzle and rain, 2 miles, 1023, rising slowly.

and that completes the Shipping Bulletin.

EXERCISES

A. Boxing de Compass

The old way of marking a card was called the point system, the card is divided in cardinal points, half cardinal points, and the three letter points, a further subdivision into by points give the thirty two points each of eleven and a quarter degrees. To name these points correctly is known as boxing the compass.

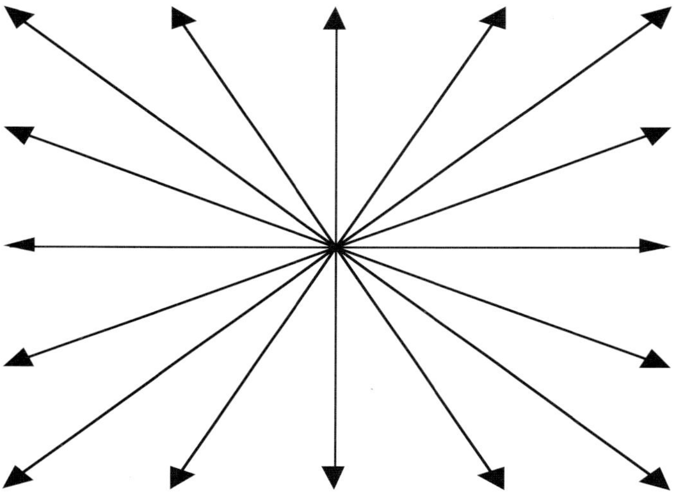

Try to write down the initials of the corresponding directions.

B. Blank Filling

After listening to the weather forecast complete the empty spaces with single words from the passage.

The Weather Forecast for the Inshore Waters of Great Britain and Northern Ireland. Until 18.00 today, Tuesday the 19th of March

A Depression will move slowly Northeast towards Southwestern areas.

From Berwick Upon Tweed to Spurn Head: Wind Easterly . . . . Southeasterly 3 or 4, occasional rain, visibility moderate or poor.

From Spurn Head to Selsey Bill: Wind Easterly 3 or 4, mainly fair, visibility moderate or . . . .: Wind Southeasterly 3 or 4, increasing 5, occasionally 6 later, mainly fair, visibility moderate or good.

From St. Davis' Head to Mull of Kyntire including Calingford Lough to Lough Foyle: Wind East or Southeast 3 or 4, ..., mainly fair, visibility moderate or poor.

From Mull of Kyntire to Cape Wrath: . . . ., occasional rain, visibility moderate or good.

From Cape Wrath to Wick including . . . .: Wind Southeasterly 4 or 5, mainly fair, visibility moderate or good.

From Wick to Berwick Upon Tweed: . . . ., occasional rain, visibility moderate or poor.

Chapter 9

The Shipping Forecast

This is Radio 4 it's 12 minutes to 1, comes now the Shipping Forecast issued by the Meteorological Office at 23-58 on Monday the 11th.of March.

There are warnings of gales in Viking, North Utsire, South Utsire, Forties, Cromarty, Forth, Tyne, Dogger, Fisher, German Bight, Humber, Lundy, Irish Sea, Malin, Hebrides, Bailey, Fair Isle, Faeroes, and Southeast Iceland.

The General Sinopsys at 18-00.

Low developing Bailey moving rather quickly North, expected 300 miles North of Iceland, 976, by 18-00 on Tuesday.

Another Low developing Fastnet, 991, by the same time.

The Area Forecast for the Next 24-00 Hours

Viking,
Southeasterly gale 8 to storm 10, wintry showers, moderate.

North Utsire, South Utsire, Forties, Cromarty, Forth,
Southeasterly 7, to severe gale 9, wintry showers, moderate occasionally poor.

Tyne, Dogger, Fisher, German Bight, Humber,
Southeasterly 6 to gale 8, wintry showers dying out, moderate.

Thames,
East or Southeast 5, increasing 6 or 7, fair, moderate.

Dover, Wight, Portland,
East or Northeast becoming Southeast 3 or 4, increasing 5 to 7, occasional rain in Wight and Portland, moderate.

Plymouth,
Southerly 4 or 5, increasing 6 or 7, perhaps gale 8 later, occasional rain, moderate or poor.

Biscay,
Southerly 3 or 4, increasing 5 to 7, veering Northwesterly in West later, rain later, moderate.

Trafalgar,
Northerly backing Westerly for a time, 4 or 5 occasionally 6, occasional rain, moderate or good.

South Finisterre,
Variable 3, becoming Southwesterly 4 or 5, occasionally 6, then veering Northerly, rain, then showers, moderate or good.

North Finisterre, Sole,
Southwesterly veering Northwesterly 5 or 6, occasionally 7, rain then showers, moderate or good.

Lundy, Fastnet, Irish Sea,
South backing Southeast 5 or 6, increasing 7, occasionally gale 8 in Lundy and Irish Sea, becoming cyclonic in Fastnet later, rain at times, moderate or poor.

Shannon, Rockall,
Southwesterly veering Northwesterly 5 to 7, rain then showers, moderate or good.

Malin,
South or Southeast 5 or 6, increasing 7 or gale 8 in Southeast later, occasional rain, moderate or good.

Hebrides,
Southerly 5 to 7, occasionally gale 8 in the North, occasional rain, moderate or good.

Bailey,
Cyclonic becoming Southwesterly 6 to gale 8, decreasing 4 or 5 later, showers, mainly good.

Fair Isle,
Southerly 7 to severe gale 9, occasionally storm 10 in the East, rain, moderate, occasionally poor.

Faeroes, Southeast Iceland,
South or Southeast becoming cyclonic at times, 6 to gale 8, wintry showers, moderate or good.

And now,
The Weather Reports from Coastal Stations for 23.00 G.M.T.

Tiree: South 6, continuous slight rain, 2 miles, 997, falling.

Stornoway: 5, continuous moderate rain, 4 miles, 998, falling.

Sumburgh: South Southeast 9, continuous moderate rain, 1.5 miles, 1008, falling slowly.

Fifeness: Southeast 8, continuous heavy rain, 1 mile, 1007, falling.

Bridlington: South by East 7, continuous slight snow, 2 miles, 1017, falling slowly.

Dover: East Southeast 6, haze, 3 miles, 1019, now rising.

Greenwich Light-Vessel Automatic: East 4, 1 mile, 1017, falling slowly.

Jersey: East 3, 1.5 miles, 1015, falling.

. . . .
. . . .
. . . .
. . . .

EXERCISES

A. **Blank Filling**

After listening to the weather forecast complete the empty spaces with single words from the passage.

This is . . . . it's 12 minutes to 1, ... the Shipping Forecast issued by the Meteorological Office at . . . . on Monday . . . . of March.

There are . . . . in Viking, North Utsire, South Utsire, Forties, Cromarty, Forth, ..., Dogger, ..., German Bight, ..., Humber, Lundy, Irish Sea, Malin, ..., Bailey, Fair Isle, ... and Southeast Iceland.

The General Sinopsys at 18-00.
. . . . Bailey. . . . . North, expected 300 miles North of Iceland, ..., by 18-00 on Tuesday.

Another . . . . Fastnet, ..., by the same time.

The Weather Reports from Coastal Stations for 23.00 G.M.T.

Tiree: South 6, ..., 2 miles, ..., falling.

Stornoway: 5, ..., 4 miles,. . . . ., falling.

. . . .: South . . . ., continuous moderate rain. 1.5 miles, 1008, ...

. . . .: Southeast 8, ..., 1 mile, 1007, falling.

Bridlington : South . . . ., continuous slight snow, ..., ..., falling slowly.

B. **Multiple Choice**

In this section you must choose the word or phrase which best completes each sentence.

1. An Artic blizzard swept through the now . . . . city streets.
   A Lonely **B** Deserted **C** Neglected **D** Insulated
2. As the sky darkened it soon become obvious that a violent thunderstrom was . . . .
   A Imminent **B** Instantaneous **C** Immediate **D** Simultaneous
3. The floods did not start to . . . . until two days after the rain stopped.
   A Retire **B** Recede **C** Retreat **D** Depart
4. The train was delayed by a heavy
   A Strike **B** Riot **C** Snowfall **D** Rebellion
5. Dry weather in the south with temperatures . . . . to normal.
   A Returning **B** Reaching **C** Achieving **D** Closing
6. Visibility moderate, with mist . . . .
   A Spells **B** Patches **C** Brisks **D** Wind
7. A strong westerly . . . . flattened the standing breakers though it brought no rain.
   A Breeze **B** Gale **C** Hurricane **D** Blizzard

Chapter 10

The Weather Forecast

Well, the heat wave continues in the southwestern United States, where it's also very dry. Folks in Pakistan and India are still waiting for the arrival of the southwest monsoons to ease their hot conditions. And, across the European continent, high pressure as clear skies have made for some very warm weather as well. There's a frontal boundary, that's moved in across the U.K., but it's not going to bring much relief to the European continent in the near future, stalled out across England at this hour.

Very low pressure in the central Mediterranean is producing a few rain showers, producing heavy rains, more than 25 milimeters or an inch, over some parts of Tunizia. And then we have a couple of fronts and throughs across western Russia, also producing some cloudiness and rain showers in that region. Saturday morning that´ll be continuing as they drop southward and eastward. Our area of low pressure in the Mediterranean moves into the Gulf of Sidra, we can see a few rain-showers along the coast of Lybia. No movement though with this frontal boundary over England, it will produce a little bit of cloudiness, and temperatures with those clouds, could be a little bit cooler in London, just 28 celsius or 82 farenheit. Still hot though from Paris over to Berlin, and rather pleasant summer-like readings across much of the continent.

On Saturday morning Africa looks very quiet as does the Middle East, just a few tropical clouds or showers. A cold front will be moving across South Africa ahead of it already some strong gusty winds reported at Cape Town, thirty or forty knots in fact, and that will produce a few rain-showers along coastal areas.

Harare on Saturday cool but sunny, Nairobi could see some rain-showers, Bangui and Abidjan could see some showers, it'll be hot and sunny Khartoum to Tel Aviv and over to Baharain.

The North American Continent is a kind of split down in the middle.

Stormy in the Eastern part of the U.S., and out across the West, we see the heat expanding to the Southwest deserts, Northwards even in to parts of Idaho on Saturday. Temperatures will be very warm with plenty of sun-shine in the west, stormy weather in the East, even Wininpeg makes it to 30 celsius, have a good day.

...Southern Argentina and Chile with rain and snow mixed there, in the vicinity of that front a little bit breezy at times. And then going well northwards on up into Venzuela, northern parts of Brazil some showers, watching a couple of waves, as they continue to move west. On up into Central America, still some rain-showers expected there. Some details include plenty of sun-shine in Ascension, we see a bit of cloud cover throughout the day on Sunday.

As it continues to move close to the coast, another tropical disturbance continuous to move northward too,this'll be moving towards Southeastern Asia, heavy rain likely in the path of that system. Elsewhere, across to Asia watching a couple of frontal systems one over South-China rain showers, thunderstorms across to Hongkong. Actually what's left over of a tropical disturbance getting absorbed into this frontal system, so there could be some significant rains over South-China and over Korea. The system likely to produce some rain-showers in Seoul. A partly sunny day expected in Tokyo. Look for thunderstorms in Hong Kong and in Colombo. Showers, thunderstorms are likely in New Delhi, a hot day, but a chance for some afternon storms.

Australia, New Zealand, a frontal system will be moving towards western sections of Australia, could see an increase in clouds and some shower chances in Perth. Another frontal system will be moving through the Great Bay region, heading into Adelaide, with some windy conditions expected along the frontal system. And over in New Zealand the weather improving with the high pressure ridge building in. Still a quite cool day in Christchurch, highs there only in the single digits, rain showers chances Adelaide, also in Sidney and in Perth, some tropical showers and storms further to the north.

Into Europe, a ridge of high pressure, bringing fair weather and warmer temperatures in through much of the Western Europe. Very nice day Sunday over the British Isle that should continue in Monday. Over Russia as polls close Sunday evening, the showers will continue over parts of Western Russia. High pressure building trough Ukraine bringing fair weather, there will be some thunderstorms though, over south eastern sections of Europe.

Into North America, we have several areas of low pressure bringing showers and storms through the plain states in the U.S. Cooler temperatures moving in to Northern U.S. from central Canada, and high pressure bringing fair weather to the North-East U.S.

EXERCISES

A. **Weather Forecast**

This is the weather forecast for the whole World. Answer these questions by choosing the best alternative (A, B, C or D).

1. Southwestern United States can expect.
   A. A very dry day.
   B. Showers and rain.
   C. A windy day.
   D. Floods and Cyclonic winds.

2. The European continent can expect.
   A. Low pressure.
   B. Clear skies.
   C. Mild temperatures.
   D. Clouded skies.

3. For Saturday morning Africa can experience.
   A. A very dry day.
   B. Some strong winds in some parts of the continent.
   C. Wind speed below twenty knots.
   D. No showers at all.

4. Southeastern Asia can expect.
   A. High pressures and clear skies.
   B. Downpours.
   C. Low temperatures.
   D. Light winds.

5. A ridge of high pressure is.
   A. An extension of an antyciclone area shown on a pressure chart.
   B. The fetch of cyclonic winds.
   C. A high possibility of precipitations.
   D. Bad weather.

B. Matching Words

Match the words under A with the meanings given under B.

A	B
1. Scattered showers	a) Moderately hot and bright.
2. Unsettled weather	b) Forepart of a weather system.
3. Very showery	c) Important water inundation.
4. Very heavy burst of rain	d) Rain with with loud noise accompanying lightning.
5. Serious flooding	e) Showers here and there.
6. Gradually dissipating	f) Inestable atmopshere.
7. Warm and sunny	g) Continuous showers.
8. Weather front	h) Downpours
9. Thundery rain	i) Slowly vanishing.

C. **Vocabulary**

Read the definitions provided, and find the corresponding technical words.

1. Region with weak pressure gradients and correspondingly light, variable winds.
2. Winds generally blowing (Beaufort 5 or 6) in latitudes 40° S to 50° S or 55° S, being the strongest at about latitude 50° S.
3. A luminous discharge of electricity from pointed objects such as masts, also known as Corposant.
4. A luminous glow appearing in varied forms in the thin atmosphere.
5. A mixture of smoke and fog.

1. □□□□□-□□□□□□□□□
2. □□□□□□□-□□□□□□□
3. □□-□□□□□-□□□□
4. □□□□□□
5. □□□□

Chapter 11

Hurricane Bertha

...Hurricane Bertha swept in on schedule, sustained winds of over 100 miles an hour sledge hammered the deserted cities and towns of North and South Carolina. Roof tiles were ripped off, streets signs blew down, sea-swells engulfed roads and trees splintered. At Wrightsville Beach in North Carolina the only sound was the fury of the wind and rain. It was a much different scene deep inside the dozens of shelters, where thousands of people are sitting the hurricane out.

Out in the swell Wrightsville pier began to give way, after a day of continual pounding, it finally collapsed.

Bertha is expected to lose strength over the next days it continues to move overland, but hurricane warnings remain in effect from South Carolina to Virginia.

EXERCISES

A. **Vocabulary**

Fill the boxes with the appropriate letter. Use a dictionary if necessary.

1. Storm. □□□□
2. Frozen vapour falling in pellets. □□□□
3. Moisture falling in drops from clouds. □□□□
4. Short fall of rain. □□□□□□
5. Violent wind or disturbence of atmosphere, adjective. □□□□□□
6. Noise accompanying lightning, adjective. □□□□□□□□
7. Very hot climate, adjective. □□□□□□□□
8. Condensed water vapour floating in air, adjective. □□□□□□
9. Gentle wind. □□□□□□
10. Mist often due to heat, poor visibility, adjective. □□□□
11. Moderately cold temperature. □□□□
12. Frozen vapour which falls in flakes. □□□□

B. Cyclones

Whenever a tropical cyclone is observed a Hurricane Warning is issued.

HURRICANE WARNINGS ARE DISPLAYED FROM KEY LARGO TO CAPE KENNEDY, GALE WARNINGS ARE DISPLAYED FROM KEY WEST TO JACKSONVILLE AND FROM FLORIDA BAY TO CEDAR KEY.

HURRICANE CENTER LOCATED NEAR LATITUD 25.5 NORTH LONGITUDE 78.5 WEST AT 21/0400Z. POSITION EXCELLENT ACCURATE WITHIN 10 MILES BASED ON AIR FORCE RECONNAISSANCE AND SYPNOTIC REPORTS.

Note the distinction between Hurricane Warning and Gale Warning, the weather and sea state expected for the last being slightly less dangerous for the navigation. All storm warnings commence with the international call sign "TTT".

Test your knowledge on cyclone-related terminology.

1. Part of a hurricane in which winds flow toward the low pressure in the warm, comparatively calm core.
2. Hurricane´s movement direction.
3. In the Northen Hemisphere, that part to the right of the storm track (facing in the direction toward which the hurricane is moving).
4. The part to the left in number 3.
5. The act of positioning on the chart the succesive positions of the storm center.
6. The expected way of the storm.
7. A wall of water caused by a hurricane which moves rapidly towards the coastline.
8. Name used in the North Western Pacific for refering to this phenomenon.
9. Local name in the Philippines for hurricanes.
10. Local name in Australia for hurricanes.

1. □□□
2. □□□□□
3. □□□□□□□□□-□□□□□□□□□□
4. □□□□□□□□□-□□□□□□□□□□
5. □□-□□□□
6. □□□□□
7. □□□□□□□□□-□□□□
8. □□□□□□□
9. □□□□□□
10. □□□□□-□□□□□

Chapter 12

The Greenhouse Effect

...the Greenhouse Effect is aptly named, Carbon Dioxide from burning oil, gas,coal and trees, forms a layer of gas in the upper atmosphere, there it absorbs reflected sunlight from the earth's surface, and as the atmosphere warms up, so does the planet. The climate of the earth is changing, it's warmer now than any time in the last 600 years. We also believe that the change we have observed, can not be ascribed to natural variability. Therefore we now believe there's a discernible human influence on the earth's climate system. And, if we don't enact global policies to restrict greenhouse gas emissions, we believe the earth's temperature will increase 1 to 3.5 degrees centigrade, over the next one hundred years.

That's a rate of change faster than anything we have observed in the last 10 thousand years. At the poles, ice caps may melt raising sea levels, the interior of North America and Eurasia may be parched, as rain-fall dries up. And violent storms could batter coastal regions. Indeed hurricanes are already causing increasing damage. A major one in the United States could land the global insurance industry with a bill for 50 billion dollars. No wonder, insurers want climate change tackled.

"We are concerned for the future, the relationship between global warming and increased claims is not yet clear cut". But, there's a growing body of opinion that says that global warming is having a major influence on the weather patterns. The weather patterns are becoming increasingly unpredictible".

...but the vested interest of oil producers and power generators are fighting back in Geneva. American industry has a powerfull pressure group.

"I think is very important to have an open and wide ranging debate on the climate issue, because the climate issue could have a tremendous economic impact". In the United States studies have shown that the issues that are being debated here, for instance a 20% reduction below 1990 levels by the year 2005, could cost the U.S. 3 to 4% G.B.P. That's not going to help the U.S., it's not going to sustain jobs, it's no going to help the world economy, because the U.S. is one of the world's drivers."

While Genevans bask in the sun-shine, civil servants have been finalizing the negociating positions. The Pacific nations threatened with oblivion sit side by side with the oil producers, who want more fossil fuel burning, not less.

The small islands states want a 20% cut in carbon dioxide emissions. The Gulf states want no cut.

It's now 4 years since world leaders first agreed to tackle global warming at the United Nations Earth-Summit in Rio.

Here in Geneva this week the 150 signatories of the Climate Change Convention meet again to discuss further cuts in carbon dioxide emissions, few have yet to meet their real commintment. But Britain has, and is keen to keep up with the work.

We got the European Union for the first time to agree to substantial reductions, those words are very important. I have not so far got them to sign up to my proposals, which are anything up to 10% reductions by the year 2010, on 1992 figures. There is only ourselves, the Luxemburgers and the Germans who have so far been specific in real ways about their reduction, and I want to get everybody else in line. But the U.K.'s progress is viewed with the scepticism by Green Groups in Geneva. Although on papers we've achieved our targets, in fact this was the result of policies which were not climate protection motivated. They were intended to, you know, destroy the coal industry.

EXERCISE

A. Questions about the Passage

Here are a number of questions about the passage, each with four suggested ways of answering. You must choose the way you consider the most suitable, and then cross through the letter of the answer you choose. Give one answer to each question. Read the passage right through again before choosing your answers.

1. Which of these details about the atmosphere is given in the passage?
   A. Carbon dioxide forms a layer.
   B. Carbon dioxide can endanger the human life.
   C. Carbon dioxide is a liquid.
   D. Carbon dioxide contributes to the earth pollution.

2. North America and Eurasia can expect.
   A. An increase in the amount of rain fallen.
   B. Mild winters.
   C. Scattered showers.
   D. A very low rate of precipitions.

3. According to the interview with the underwriter on the second paragrah of page 54.
   A. There is a clear relation between global warming and insurance claims.
   B. The weather patterns are known much better nowadays.
   C. The man felt very disappointed.
   D. The man thought that the weather pattern is quite unpredictable.

4. As a result of the Geneva meeting the small islands demand.
   A. A drastical cut of the carbon dioxide emissions to the atmosphere.
   B. To reduce one fifth of the carbon dioxide emissions.
   C. A mere 10 per cent reduction in the carbon dioxide emissions.
   D. To reduce the sales of oil.

5. What is the main reason why the British politician is trying to convince other UE members of his proposals.

A. He knows that Britain has already achieved the targets.
B. Other UE members are reluctant to agree to his porposals.
C. The back of the Luxemburgers and the Germans makes him feel confident.
D. Green Groups are very demanding.

B. **Blank Filling**

Fill each of the blanks in the following passage with one suitable word.

The greenhouse effect . . . . the air, for example, so that it can . . . . more water vapour, but water vapour . . . . is a powerfull greenhouse gas. So it exarcebates the . . . . If the sea ice . . . ., the colloing effect it would otherwise supply is gone. Dying trees become a source of . . . ., rather than a consumer of it. And so on. The scientists in charge of long-term . . . ., say that the work done clearly shows that . . . . activities are, in fact, causing the . . . . in temperatures. This is, of course, the part of science that people argue . . . . most.

Chapter 13

The Weather Forecast

Good afternoon, for a change it's not more of the same as today the cloud is thinner and more broken, with many places seeing sun-shine and better temperatures, as a result, mind you, it doesn't mean that there is eh! sorry, mind you it does mean that'll be some frost about tonight. Now, some areas probably won't see that much sun-shine and so let's look at those first of all, and they are Southeast and Central Southern England, The Midlands, SouthWales, East Anglia, Northeast England and then jumping up to Northern Scotland. I am not ruling out sun-shine altogether, especially in the Midlands and around London, but, most of these parts will stay fairly cloudy and in Norfolk, the Hebrides, Highland regions and the Northern Isles there the cloud will be thick enough to give a few spots of drizzle. Temperatures will be close to normal, that's touching 9 degrees this afternoon.

Tonight most of these parts will cloud over again, any holes that developed this afternoon filling in. It 'll start dry, but later on tonight, light rain or drizzle will spread from the East into Eastern parts of England and from the North into Northern Scotland. Over the hills of the Southeast like for instance the Downs and Chilterns, the rain may well turn to sleet, temperatures will fall to 2 degrees and acros East Anglia, the East Midland, and Southeast England, winds will freshen from the Northeast.

Now, for Southwest England and the Channel Islands, probably staying cloudy here, both today and for much of the night, although there could be some breaks in the cloud for a time this evening and at first tonight.

Temperatures this afternoon will be around 8 degrees, it'll probably fall close to freezing in-land tonight, with a touch of frost during the time that the cloud breaks. And now, let's head to the sunshine, with North Wales, Northwest England, Northern Ireland, and Southern Scotland, dry with a reasonable amount of sun-shine across these parts, and with light wind it should feel almost like spring-like, as temperatures will touch ten degrees. Cloud will remain well broken for much of the night, with the result that temperatures will fall to around freezing and there could well be a touch of frost, and a few fog patches, but later on in the night, it will tend to cloud over again in North Wales and Northwest England and temperatures here will rise a shade.

Tomorrow, England. Wales, and Eastern Scotland will be rather cloudy with some patchy rain or drizzle and there will still be some sleet over the hills, but all this will tend to probably gradually die out during the course of the day.

Northern Ireland and Western Scotland will be dry with sunny spells, and it's going to start to feel much colder specially in Eastern parts of the country, as a strong easterly wind picks up.

EXERCISES

A. True or False Statements

After carefully listening to the weather forecast, study the following sentences and state wether they are true or false according to the information in the text.

	T	F
1. There is a slight chance of sunshine in the Midlands.	☐	☐
2. Highland regions can expect heavy rains.	☐	☐
3. Norfolk can expect drizzle.	☐	☐
4. At Chilterns heavy snow storms are experienced.	☐	☐
5. East Anglia will experience temperatures below zero.	☐	☐
6. The weather could slightly improve during the evening.	☐	☐
7. Temperatures close to freezing are expected in coastal areas.	☐	☐
8. North Wales can expect a quite nice day with some sunshine.	☐	☐
9. A summer-like day can be expected in Northwest England.	☐	☐
10. During the night overcast skies can be expected in Northern Ireland.	☐	☐
11. For tomorrow snow is expected for Eastern Scotland.	☐	☐
12. A gradual increase of temperatures is forecasted in Wales.	☐	☐
13. North Ireland will enjoy a day through sunshine.	☐	☐
14. The Eastern parts of the country will experience a cool day.	☐	☐

Chapter 14

The Weather Forecast

The mostly wet afternoon in the North and Northwestern parts will slowly brighten. Wales Northern and Western England meanwhile, largely overcast with rain moving in later. South and Central England on the cloudy side as well, but will stay dry there with some sunny spells.

Tonight England and Wales will see patchy rain spreading from the Northwest rain will die out as it edges South, so although Southeast England will cloud over later, it will stay dry. Clear settled weather over Scotland and Ireland meanwhile will lead to a touch of frost.

EXERCISES

A. Matching Words

Match the words under list A with the meanings given under list B.

A	B
1. wet	a) Having the qualities of a certain season of year.
2. bright	b) Full of patches, spots here and there.
3. overcast	c) To extinguish.
4. sunny spells	d) Rain and snow or hail falling together.
5. settled weather	e) Small areas of light rain.
6. frost	f) To replace something (in meteorology).
7. sleet	g) Winds blowing from a certain direction for a period.
8. patchy	h) Course of ship obliquely to windward.
9. parched	i) Weather in which temperature falls below cero.
10. to die out	j) Capacity for endurance.
11. to fill in	k) Alert for winds at least Beaufourt force 8.
12. spring-like	l) Hot and dry.
13. spots of drizzle	m) Seasonal wind of the Indian ocean.
14. to tack	n) Calm weather.
15. eddy	o) Covered with clouds.
16. sustained winds	p) Being soaked.
17. strength	q) Wind whirling round forward.
18. gale warning	r) Shining, full of light.
19. monsoon	s) Wind direction changing clock-wise.
20. veering	t) Sunny intervals.

Chapter 15

The Weather Forecast

The United Kingdom for Wednesday, the Midlands, East Anglia, Central Southern, and Southeast England will have a better day with some brighter weather after a misty start, a few pockets of rain may spread from the West later.

Southwest England, Wales and Northern England will start off dry but thickening cloud will bring some light rain through the morning and this will become more persistent later.

Scotland and Northern Ireland will soon become wet and windy with brighter weather then arriving through the afternoon, scattered showers are likely in the Northwest and these will turn wintry later. Most places will be mild.

And the outlook for both Thursday and Friday, wind and rain will spread to Northern and Western areas followed by brighter showery weather. Southern and Eastern areas will be mostly dry with brighter spells and that´s the forecast.

EXERCISES

A. True or False Statements

After carefully listening to the weather forecast, study the following sentences and state whether they are true or false according to the information in the text.

		T	F
1.	A better weather can be expected for North Anglia.	☐	☐
2.	A dry day is forecasted for the Midlands.	☐	☐
3.	Some cloudiness and rain is forecasted for Wales.	☐	☐
4.	Northern Ireland will experience a rapid weather deterioration.	☐	☐
5.	Reasonable temperatures can be expected for the northwest.	☐	☐
6.	An improvement can be expected for the southern area.	☐	☐

B. Match the Front Types with their Corresponding Symbols and Colour Codes

Type	Symbol		Colour Code
Cold front (a)		(1)	Dashed Blue Line +
Warm front (b)		(2)	Blue Line *
Stationary front (c)		(3)	Purple Line #
Upper cold front (d)	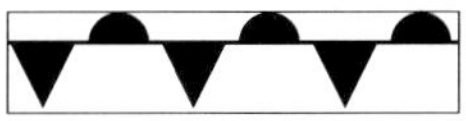	(4)	Red Line @
Occluded front (e)	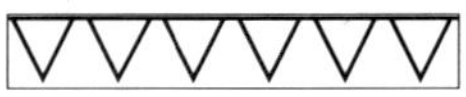	(5)	Alternate Red and Blue &

C. **Vocabulary**

Read the definitions provided, and find the corresponding technical word.

1. The highest part of waves.
2. The lowest part of waves.
3. The vertical distance between through and crest.
4. The horizontal distance between succesive crests.
5. The time interval between passage of successive crests at a stationary point.
6. The straight distance that the wave has traveled over the surface.
7. Waves generated by the blowing wind.
8. Waves generated by a previous wind.
9. Swell passing over a shoal but no breaking.
10. Unstable wave, with the faster moving top falling or breaking.

1. □□□□□
2. □□□□□□□
3. □□□□□□
4. □□□□□□□□□□
5. □□□□□□□□□□
6. □□□□□
7. □□□
8. □□□□□
9. □□□□
10. □□□□□□

R. MET.SOC. / R.Y.A. METMAP (Revised Feb 1986)

GENERAL SYPNOSIS at . . . . GMT/BST . . . .

Gale	SEA AREA FORECAST		Wind	Weather	Visibility
	Viking				
	N. Utsire				
	S. Utsire				
	Forties				
	Cromarty				
	Forth				
	Tyne				
	Dogger				
	Fisher				
	German Bight				
	Humber				
	Thames				
	Dover				
	Wight				
	Portland				
	Plymouth				
	Biscay				
	Finisterre				
	Sole				
	Lundy				
	Fastnet				
	Irish Sea				
	Shannon				
	Rockall				
	Malin				
	Hebrides				
	Bailey				
	Fair Isle				
	Faeroes				
	SE. Iceland				

* Mark gale areas * Connect areas grouped in forecast

COASTAL REPORTS Shipping Bulletin At . . . . GMT/BST	Wind		Weather	Visibili.	Pressure	Trend
	Direc	Force				
Tiree						
Butt of Lewis						
Sumburgh						
Bell Rock						
Dowsing						
Dover						
Royal Sovereign						
Channel L.V.						
Scilly						
Valentia						
Ronaldsway						
Malin Head						
Jersey						

COASTAL REPORTS Inshore Waters At . . . . GMT/BST	Wind		Weather	Visibili.	Pressure	Trend
	Direc	Force				
Boulmer						
Spurn Head						
Walton on the Naze						
St. Catherine's Point						
Land's End						
Mumbles						
Valley						
Blackpool						
Prestwick						
Benbecula						
Stornoway						
Lerwick						
Wick						
Aberdeen						
Leuchars						

Glossary of Terms

Air Mass: A mass of air which is largely homogeneous in a horizontal direction.

Anemometer: Instrument for determining the speed of the wind.

Antyciclone: Also known as "high", barometric pressure distribution characterized by a system of closed isobars.

Backing: Change in the directions of the wind, in an anti-clockwise direction.

Blind rollers: The name given to the swell resulting from a very distant storm.

Blizzard: A high wind accompanied by great cold and drifting snow.

B.S.T.: British standard ti me.

Breakers: Waves or swell which have become so steep, either on reaching shoal water or on encountering a contrary current or by wind action.

Breaking Sea: "WHITE HORSES", The partial collapse of the crest of waves.

Cloud: Clouds are aggregates of minute water drops or ice chrystals held in suspension in the atmosphere. For practical purposes are classified into 4 main groups: *High Clouds, Medium Clouds, Low Clouds, and Low Clouds with a marked vertical extent.*

Cold Front: The boundary line between the advancing cold air and the rear of a depression and the warm sector. It was formerly called the squall line.

Cold Sector: That part of a depression occupied by cold air on the earth's surface.

Cross-Sea: A wave formation imposed across the prevailing winds

Cross swell: Similar to Cross-Sea but the waves are longer swell waves.

Cyclone: A name given to tropical cyclones of the Bay of Bengal and the Arabian Sea. Sometimes used for tropical cyclones of all oceans. First experienced by the Spaniards while sailing Central American Waters.

Dangerous Quadrant: The forward quadrant of the dangerous semicircle of a cyclone, which before recurvature is nearer the pole in both hemispheres.

Depression: A region characterized in the barometric distribution by a system of closed isobars, having lowest pressure on the inside.

Dew Point: The temperature to which air can be cooled without causing condensation.

Diurnal Variation: This term is used to indicate the changes, in the course of an average day, in the magnitude of a meteorological element.

Drift: To move along with the current, tidal stream, or wind or under all of these.

Drift Current: A horizontal movement in the upper layers of the sea, caused by the wind.

Eddy: A name given to the deviation from the steady motion which occurs in any viscous fluid which flows past an obstacle or in which neighbouring streams flow past over each other. Air and water eddies

The Equatorial Trough (Doldrums): Is an area of low pressure situated between the Trade Winds of the two hemispheres. Characteristic features of this area are light and variable winds alternating with squalls, heavy rain and thunderstorms. The Trough varies greatly in width both daily and seasonally. The type of weather experienced also varies considerably. At times a ship may cross the Trough and experience fine weather, while on another crossing squalls and thunderstorms may be encountered: Weather in the Trough is generally worst when the Trade winds are strongest. This is a highly simplified account of an area where the weather is complicated and not completely understood.

Eye of Storm: The calm, central area of a tropical cyclone.

Fetch: The distance a sea wave has travelled to the observer from the locality of the wind that caused it or from the nearest weather shore.

Fog: Is a cloud in the surface, and is specified according to the visibility which it allows. When fog is experienced there will be little or no differences beween the readings of the dry and wet bulb thermometers

Following Sea: One running in the same direction as the ship is steering.

Gap: A break in a ridge or rise.

Ground Swell: A swell which, on reaching dephts of less than half its length, becomes shorter and steeper.

Gust: A comparatively rapid fluctuation in the strength of the wind, characteristic of the winds near the surface of the earth.

Hail: Hard pellets of ice, of various shapes and sizes.

Horse Latitudes: Zones of high pressure with calms and variable breezes, which border the polar edges of the Trade wind areas in the North hemisphere.

Hurricane: A name given to the tropical cyclone of the West Indian region. Also applied to force 12 in the Beaufort scale, whatever its cause.

Isobars: Lines drawn through positions having the same barometric pressure, when reduced to sea level

Monsoons: Seasonal winds, those in the Indian Ocean, China Sea, and off the West Coast of Africa. Over certain parts of the oceans the general distribution of pressure and wind is greatly modified by the seasonal heating and cooling of adjacent large land masses. The annual range of sea temperature in the open ocean is comparatively small, whereareas large land masses become hot in summer and cold in winter. The alternate heating and cooling of the land results in the formation of areas of low and high pressure respectively. This redistribution of pressure results in a seasonal reversal of the prevailing wind over the adjacent oceans. The most important ocean areas subject to these seasonal winds are Indian Ocean, West Pacific Ocean and those adjacent to the coast of West Africa.

Ocean Swell: A swell encountered in the open ocean in great depths.

Occlussion: When the whole of the warm sector of a depresssion has been pushed up from the earth's surface by the advance of the cold front behind it, this is known as an occlusion, and the depression in which it occurs is called an occluded depression.

Psychrometer: The dry-and-wet bulb hygrometer

Rainbow: An arch of coloured light in the sky, made by rain drops breaking up the white light of the sun into its component colours.

Recurvature of Storm: Recurvature of the track of a tropical cyclone.

Ridge: An extension of an antyciclone or high-pressure area shown on a pressure chart, corresponding with a ridge running out from from the side of a mountain.

Sea Breezes: During the day-time the lan is warmer that the sea and a breeze, the sea-breeze, blows onshore.

Shower: The clouds which give the showers are isolated. The precipitation does not usually last more than 15 minutes, though it may occasionally last for half an hour or more.

Sleet: precipitation of snow and rain together, or of melting snow.

Snow: Precipitation of ice crystals or flakes.

Squall: A strong wind that rises suddenly, last for a few minutes, and dies away rapidly.

Storm Signals: Visual warnings of bad weather in the form of cones or flags and lights, displayed at certain stations on the coast and in harbours.

Storm Surge: A progressive wave of meteorological origin which, if its crest arrives at the time of high water, can cause exceptionally high tides.

Surge: The difference in height between predicted and observed tides due to abnormal weather conditions.

Swell: This is a wave motion in the ocean caused by a disturbance which may be at some distance away; the swell may persist after the originating cause of the wave motion has passed away.

Thunder: The noise made by an electric discharge (lightning).

Through: Is the line, throughout the centre, perpendicular to the line of advance of the centre.

Typhoon: A name given to the tropical cyclones of the China Sea and the West Part of the Pacific Ocean.

Veering: A change in the direction of the wind, in a clockwise direction.

Warm Sector, Warm Front: Most depressions in their earlier stages, have an area of warm air on the side nearest the equator, known as the warm sector. The warm front is the boundary between the front of the warm sector, as the depression advances, and the colder air in front of it.

Waterspout: Phenomenon in which a cloud forms a funnel-shaped pendant which descends towards the sea and draws up a corresponding hollow column of whirling spray which may form a pillar of water from cloud to the sea, the whole travelling across the surface of the sea.

Wind: Because of the rotation of the earth, air which is drawn towards a centre of low pressure is deflected to the right in the N hemisphere and to the left in the S hemisphere.

Wind drift current: A horizonal movement in the upper layers of the sea, caused by the wind.

Weather and Climate

What's the weather like?

Hot, sunny, boiling hot, hot, cold, freezing cold, wet, humid, cool, sticky, warm, nice, fine, dull, rainy, cloudy, windy, breezy, stormy, misty, showery, foggy, thundery, drizzly.

Verbs

To be hot, to be cold, to be sunny, to be drizzly, to be drizzling, to pelt (rain), to pour with rain, to snow, to rain, to rain heavily, to freeze, to melt (snow), to frost, to overcast, to spread (clouds), to hail, to freeze.

Nouns

Wind
A light wind, a strong wind, a high wind, a gust of wind, windforce.

Rain
Heavy/light rain, shower, downpour, squall.

Fog
Thick fog, fog bank.

Snow
Heavy/light snow, sleet.

Drizzle
Light drizzle (also thin drizzle).

Shower
Heavy/light shower.

Clouds
High/thick clouds.

Breeze
A gentle/light breeze.

Spells
Sunny Spells all over Britain.

Gale Warnings

These are issued only when winds of at least force "8" or gusts reaching 43 kn. to 51 kn. are expected. "Severe Gale" implies winds of at least force "9" or gusts reaching 52 kn. to 60 kn. "Storm" implies a mean wind of at least force "10" or gusts reaching at least 61 Kn. to 68 Kn. Imminent implies within 6 hours of the time of issue. "Soon" implies between 6 and 12 hours. "Later" implies more that 12 hours.

Gale warnings remain in force unless amended or cancelled. However, if the gale persists for more than 24 hours after the time of origin, the warning will be re-issued.

Shipping Forecast Terminology

Gale Warnings

GALE: Winds of at least Beaufourt force 8 (34-40 knots) or gusts reaching 43-51 knots.

SEVERE GALE: Winds of force (41-47 knots) or gusts reaching 52-60 knots.

VIOLENT STORM: Winds of force 11 (56-63 knots) or gusts of 69 knots or more.

HURRICANE FORCE: Winds of force 12 (64 knots or more). The term hurricane on its own is only used to imply a true tropical cyclone.

INMINENT: Expected within 6 hours of time of issue.
SOON: Expected within 6 to 12 hours of time of issue.
LATER: Expected more than 12 hours from time of issue.

Visibility

FOG: Visibility less than 1000 m.
POOR: Visibility between 1000 m. and 2 nautical miles.
MODERATE: Visibility between 2 and 5 nautical miles.
GOOD: Visibility more than 5 nautical miles.

Movement of Pressure Systems

SLOWLY: Moving at less than 15 knots.
STEADILY: Moving at 15 to 25 knots.
RATHER QUICKLY: Moving at 25 to 35 knots.
RAPIDLY: Moving at 35 to 45 knots.
VERY RAPIDLY: Moving at more than 45 knots.

Pressure Tendency in Station Reports

RISING OR FALLING MORE SLOWLY: Pressure change of 0.1 to 1.5 hPa in the preceding 3 hours.
RISING OR FALLING SLOWLY: Pressure change of 1.6 to 3.5 hPa in the preceding 3 hours.
RISING OR FALLING QUICKLY: Pressure change of 3.6 to 6.0 hPa in the preceding 3 hours.
RISING OR FALLING VERY RAPIDLY: Pressure change of more than 6.0 hPa in the preceding 3 hours.
NOW RISING OR FALLING: Pressure has been falling (rising) or steady in the preceding 3 hours, but at the time of observation was definitely rising or (falling).

Wind

WIND DIRECTION: Indicates the direction from which the wind is blowing.

WIND BECOMING CYCLONIC: Indicates that there will be considerable change in wind direction across the path of a depression within the forecast area.

VEERING: The changing of the wind in the direction of motion of the hands of a clock, e.g. SW to W.

BACKING: The opposite direction to veering, e.g. SE to NE.

Beaufort scale of wind force

Beaufort Wind Force	Mean Wind Speed in knots Measured of 10 m.	Limits of Wind Speed in knots at a height above sea level	Descriptive Term	Sea Criterion	Probable height of Waves in Metres	Probable Maximum Height of Waves in Metres
0	00	Less than 1	Calm	Sea like a mirror	0	0
1	02	1-3	Light air	Ripples with the appearance of scales are formed, but without foam crests.	0	0.1
2	05	4-6	Light breeze	Small wavelets, still short but more pronounced, crest have a glassy appearance and do not break.	0.1	0.3
3	09	7-10	Gentle breeze	Large wavelets. Crets begin to break. Foam of glassy appearance. Perhaps scattered with horses.	0.4	1.0
4	13	11-16	Moderate breeze	Small waves, becoming longer, fairly frequent white horses.	1.0	1.5
5	19	17-21	Fresh breeze	Moderate waves, taking a more pronounced long form; many white horses are formed. Chance of some spray.	2.0	2.5
6	24	22-27	Strong breeze	Large waves begin to form; the white foam crests are more extensive everywhere. Probably some spray.	3.0	4.0
7	30	28-33	Near gale	Sea heaps up and white foam from breaking waves begings to be blown in streaks along the direction of the wind.	4.0	5.5
8	37	34-40	Gale	Moderately-high waves of greater length; edges of crests begin to break into spindrift. The foam is blown in well-marked streaks along the direction of the wind.	5.5	7.5
9	44	41-47	Strong gale	High waves. Dense streaks of foam along the direction of the wind. Crests of waves begin to topple, tumble and roll over. Spray may affect visibility.	7.0	10.0
10	52	48-55	Storm	Very hight waves with long overhanging crests. The resulting foam in great patches is blown in dense white streaks along the direction of the wind. On the whole the surface of the sea takes a white appearance. Tumbling of the sea becomes heavy and shock-like. Visibility affected.	9.0	12.5
11	60	56-63	Violent storm	Exceptionally-high waves (small and medium-sized ships might be for a time lost of view behind the waves). The sea is completely covered with long white patches of foam lying along the direction of the wind. Everywhere the edges of the waves' crests are blown into froth. Visibility affected.	11.5	16.05
12	—	64 and over	Hurricane force	The air is filled with foam and spray. Sea completely white with driving spray. Visibility very seriously affected.	14 or over	—

These columns are added as a guide to show roughly what may be expected in the open sea, remote from land. In enclosed waters, or whe near and with an offshore wind, wave heights will be smaller, and the waves steeper.

Notes. (1) It must be realised that it may be difficult to estimate wind force by sea criterion. The wind force and direction may therefore b estimated by other means, e.g. the "feel" of the wind or the smoke, making due allowance for course and speed of ship.

(2) The lag effect between the wind getting up and the sea increasing should be borne in mind.

(3) Fetch, depth, swell, heavy rain and tide effects should be considered when estimating the wind force from the appearance of the sea

Force 0

Force 1

Force 2

Force 3

Force 4

Force 5

Force 6

Force 7

Force 8

Force 9

Force 10

Force 11

Force 12

Meteorological Codes

These tables are based on the International Meteorological Code. When necessary, to amplify the "States of Weather", reference should be made to the appropiate section in the "Marine Observer's Handbook", which, together with the Code, is supplied to all vessels.

SEA (Douglas Scale)

		Ht.	Feet
0	Calm	0	
1	Smooth	0	1/2
2	Slight	1/2	2
3	Moderate	2	5
4	Rough	5	9
5	Very Rough	9	15
6	High	15	24
7	Very High	24	36
8	Precipitious	Over 36	
9	Confused	...	...

SWELL (Douglas Scale)

0	No Swell
1	Low Swell, Short or Average Length
2	Low Swell, Long
3	Moderate Swell, Short
4	Moderate Swell, Average Length
5	Moderate Swell, Long
6	Heavy Swell, Short
7	Heavy Swell, Average Length
8	Heavy Swell, Long
9	Confused Swell

Fog and Visibility scale

0	Dense Fog	Vis. less than 50 yards
1	Thick Fog	50 yards to 1 cable
2	Fog	1 cable to 2 cable
3	Moderate Fog	2 cables to 1/2 mile
4	Mist or Haze	1/2 mile to 1 mile
5	Poor Visibility	1 mile to 2 miles
6	Moderate Visibility	2 miles to 5 miles
7	Good Visibility	5 miles to 10 miles
8	Very Good Visibility	10 miles to 30 miles
9	Excellent Visibility	More than 30 miles

State of Weather

Blue Sky
Sky Partly Clouded
Cloudy
Drizzle
Wet Air (Without Precipitation)
Fog
Gale
Hail
Precipitation in Sight of Ship
Line Squall
Storm of Drifting Snow
Sandstorm or Dust Storm
Lightning
Mist
Overcast Sky (Sky completely covered)
Squally Weather
Rain
Sleet (Rain and Snow together)
Snow
Thunder
Thunderstorm with Rain

Thunderstorm with Snow
Ugly Threatening Sky
Unusual Visibility
Dew
Hoar Frost
Dry Air
Haze

Weather Phenomena

WIND. Calm. Gentle breeze. Breeze. Light breeze. Breezy. Light Wind. Strong wind. High wind. Gust of wind. Wind force. Windy. Wintry. Wet air. Blizzard.

RAIN. Drizzle. Light drizzle. Thin drizzle. To be drizzly. To pelt. To pour with rain. Down-pours. To rain. To rain heavily. Rainy weather. Hail. To hail. Sleet. Shower. Showery. Scattered showers. To be soaked. Torrential down-pour. Wet. Precipitations in sight. Line squall.

SKY. Blue sky. Partly clouded. Cloudy. Overcast. High clouds. Medium clouds. Low clouds. Low clouds of marked vertical extent. Ugly, threatening sky. Scud.

FOG. Fog patches. Foggy weather. Haze. Hazy weather. Dust haze. Mist. Misty weather. Smog. Fog banks. Sea smoke. Radiation fog. Advocation fog.

Hurricane

No one knows for sure exactly what goes into the making of a hurricane. Below are some basic ingredients. We use size to guess what influences the cretion and growth of a hurricane. But in real life size isn´t necessary linked to a hurricane´s ferocity.

* Water must be at least 80 degrees Farenheit. Storms can grow rapidly in size and strength when the water temperatures are higher than this.

* Strong high-altitude winds, actin like an exhaust system, are needed to push rising hot air away from the storm. However, forceful shearing winds, moving at different speeds and directions at different heights, can disrupt a hurricane´s formation or rip apart and existing one.

* Significant differences in air pressure over distance, called a pressure gradient, drive the hurricane´s growth as air rushes toward the low-pressure center of the storm. The steeper the gradient, the faster the wind blows.

* Warm and moist air carries evaporated water from the ocean upward into the sky, like an escalator. As the moist air irses and cools, it condenses into rain and releases heat in the process, causing more air to rise and fueling the growth of the storm.

* The spin, due to the Earth´s rotation and a byproduct called the Coriolis Effect, gives the hurricane its characteristic pinwheel shape and is a key to a hurricane´s start. Hurricanes won´t develop within 5 degrees latitud of the equator, because the Coriolis effect is too weak there to give hurricanes enough twist.

Answer Key

Exercise 1

True or false statements.

1 T, 2 T, 3 F, 4 F, 5 F, 6 F.

Exercise 2

Blank filling.

In the text.

True or false statements.

1 T, 2 F, 3 F, 4 T, 5 T, 6 T. Northern sea areas refers to Hebrides, Bailey, Fair Isle, Faeroes, and Southeast Iceland.

Matching words.

1 h, 2 g, 3 k, 4 f, 5 i, 6 l, 7 e, 8 b, 9 d, 10 j, 11 a, 12 c.

Exercise 3

The missing letters.

Shine, weather, bed and breakfast, path, light-house, visibility, stratus, drizzle, hail, gales, temperature, data, supply, Post Office, tower, sunlight.

True or false statements.

1 F, 2 T, 3 T, 4 F, 5 F, 6 T, 7 T, 8 T, 9 T, 10 F.

Vocabulary.

1 Cirrus, 2 Cirrocumulus, 3 Altostratus, 4 Cumulus, 5 Cumulonimbus.

Exercise 4

Dialogue.

Radio Call. about, sea, drastically, impossible, called, waves, forecast, wrong, threatening, sense, set off, sky, happening, situation, coastguards.

Matching words.

1 f, 2 e, 3 a, 4 b, 5 h, 6 c, 7 g, 8 d.

Exercise 5

Weather forecast.

1 C, 2 A, 3 C, 4 C, 5 C.

Multiple choice questions.

1 B, 2 A, 3 B, 4 C, 5 D, 6 D, 7 B.

Exercise 6

Matching words.

1 o, 2 e, 3 f, 4 g, 5 k, 6 r, 7 h, 8 m, 9 p, 10 c, 11 a, 12 n, 13 q, 14 i, 15 d, 16 b, 17 l, 18 t, 19 r, 20 s.

Weather Report form filling.

In the text.

Vocabulary.

1 Apparent wind, 2 Anemometer, 3 Farenheit, 4 Absolute zero, 5 Dewpoint, 6 Haze, 7 Hygrometer, 8 Doldrums, 9 Trade winds, 10 Coriolis.

Exercise 7

Shipping forecast terminology.

Gale, hurricane force, inminent, later, fog, poor, good.

Blank filling.

In the text.

Exercise 8

Boxing the compass.

Clockwise sequence. north, north northeast, northeast, east northeast, east, east southeast. southeast, south southeast, south,

south southwest, southwest, west southwest, west, west northwest, northwest, north northwest.

The smaller divisions, the points each of eleven and a quarter degree have been omitted. Example from north to northeast would be, north, north by east, north northeast, northeast by north, northeast.

Blank filling.

In the text.

Exercise 9

Blank filling.

In the text.

Multiple choice questions.

1 B, 2 C, 3 B, 4 C, 5 A, 6 B, 7 B.

Exercise 10

Multiple choice questions.

1 A, 2 B, 3 B, 4 B, 5 A.

Matching words.

1 e, 2 f, 3 g, 4 h, 5 c, 6 i, 7 a, 8 b, 9 d.

Vocabulary.

1 Horse latitudes, 2 Roaring forties, 3 St. Elmo´s fire, 4 Aurora, 5 Smog.

Exercise 11

Vocabulary.

1 Gale, 2 Hail, 3 Rain, 4 Shower, 5 Stormy, 6 Thundery, 7 Tropical, 8 Cloudy. 9 Breeze, 10 Hazy, 11 Cool, 12 Snow.

Cyclones.

1 Eye, 2 Track, 3 Dangerous semicircle, 4 Navigable semicircle, 5 To plot, 6 Path, 7 Hurricane wave, 8 Typhoon, 9 Baguio, 10 Willy-willy.

Exercise 12

Questions about the passage.

1 A, 2 D, 3 D, 4 B, 5 A.

Blank filling.

In the text.

Exercise 13

True or false statements.

1 T, 2 F, 3 T, 4 F, 5 F, 6 T, 7 F, 8 T, 9 F, 10 F, 11 F, 12 T, 13 F, 14 T.

Exercise 14

Matching words.

1 p, 2 r, 3 o, 4 t, 5 n, 6 i, 7 d, 8 b, 9 l, 10 c, 11 f, 12 a, 13 e, 14 h, 15 q, 16 g, 17 j, 18 k, 19 m, 20 s.

Exercise 15

True or false statements.

1 F, 2 F, 3 T, 4 T, 5 T, 6 T.

Front types and simbols.

a 1 *, b 3 @, c 4 &, d 5 +, e 2 #.

Vocabulary.

1 Crest, 2 Through, 3 Height, 4 Wavelength, 5 Wave period, 6 Fetch, 7 Sea, 8 Swell, 9 Surf, 10 Breaker.

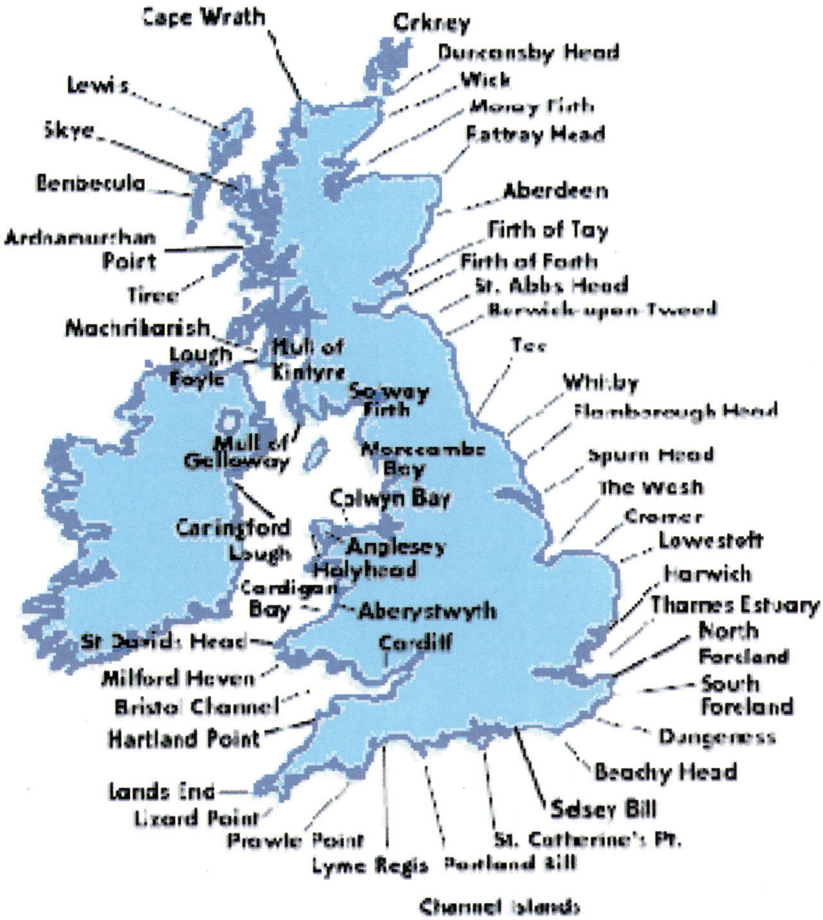
Cape Wrath
Orkney
Duncansby Head
Wick
Moray Firth
Rattray Head
Lewis
Skye
Benbecula
Aberdeen
Ardnamurchan Point
Firth of Tay
Firth of Forth
St. Abbs Head
Tiree
Berwick-upon-Tweed
Machrihanish
Tee
Lough Foyle
Mull of Kintyre
Whitby
Solway Firth
Flamborough Head
Mull of Galloway
Morecambe Bay
Spurn Head
The Wash
Colwyn Bay
Cromer
Carlingford Lough
Lowestoft
Anglesey
Holyhead
Harwich
Cardigan Bay
Aberystwyth
Thames Estuary
St Davids Head
Cardiff
North Foreland
Milford Haven
South Foreland
Bristol Channel
Hartland Point
Dungeness
Beachy Head
Lands End
Selsey Bill
Lizard Point
Prawle Point
St. Catherine's Pt.
Lyme Regis
Portland Bill
Channel Islands

Moscow
Oslo
Kiev
London
Paris
Rome
Athens
Lisbon
Tenerife
MONDAY 1600